FIRST-TIME
GARDENER

To anyone starting out on their gardening voyage. May it bring you as much joy as it has brought me. Good luck!

First published in Great Britain
in 2015 by Kyle Books an imprint of
Kyle Cathie Limited
192–198 Vauxhall Bridge Road
London SW1V 1DX
general.enquiries@kylebooks.com
www.kylebooks.com

10 9 8 7 6 5 4 3 2 1

ISBN: 978 0 85783 254 2

A CIP catalogue record for this title is available from the British Library

Editor **Vicky Orchard**
Design **Helen Bratby**
Photography **Clare Winfield**
Illustration **Esther Coombs**
Production **Lisa Pinnell**

Colour reproduction by ALTA London
Printed and bound in China by
C&C Offset Printing Co., Ltd

Frances Tophill

FIRST-TIME GARDENER

how to plan, plant & enjoy your garden

Photography by Clare Winfield

Kyle Books

CONTENTS

N
E
S
W
Jan Feb
HB
BOURBON

CHAPTER 1

YOU & YOUR GARDEN

WHAT HAVE YOU INHERITED?

OK, so you've just moved into your own place and have a plot of land that you have absolutely no idea what to do with... Well, the first thing to remember is don't panic – a garden that's a bit unruly or somewhat bare is not disastrous. With a little patience and perseverance, you'll be able to transform your uninspiring, inherited plot into a magical, personalised haven that you, your family and friends will enjoy for many years to come.

Although it can be tempting to make improvements straightaway, it's much better to get to know the existing garden before making any alterations. Use the first few months of living in your new home to focus on jobs that require immediate attention in and around the house, while keeping a keen eye on what's happening outside. Remember, the landscape changes continually, and the garden may throw up surprises as the seasons change: there may be hidden treasures beneath the bare ground that will rear their heads only at certain times of the year, or you may discover that the huge bush you were thinking of removing does in fact earn its place after all – perhaps it produces a mass of stunning, fragrant flowers, or serves a practical purpose such as stopping the neighbour's kids climbing into your garden. There may be a small unkempt corner that is a haven for wildlife, which you don't want to disrupt unnecessarily. I would recommend that at least the first year should be spent becoming familiar with the garden before getting stuck into any rebuild project – just do what you can to keep the vegetation under control if necessary.

You may have moved into a home with an immaculate garden but it is not to your taste, or you know you couldn't keep up with the maintenance required. If you feel guilty or nervous at the thought of making any big alterations, don't be. After all, it is your garden now, so do as you wish.

At the other end of the spectrum, you may find the garden is nothing but soil and rubble, particularly if you're in a new build. Although a blank canvas can seem intimidating at first, it has many advantages in the long run, as it allows you to create a garden that is entirely your own.

You may have features like an old pond or shed that can be vastly improved with a bit of TLC or a lick of paint (right).

ASSESS YOUR SITE

One of the first things you need to do in your new garden, before making any changes, is a site survey. This may sound daunting, but the vast majority of it can be done through simple observation, and what can't is still incredibly easy to carry out. Below are some key attributes that it really pays to consider at the planning stage.

1. Setting

The setting should inform your design. The house – your house, that is – will affect the overall look of your garden. Creating a smooth transition from house to garden will create a finished, more cohesive look. An easy way to achieve this is to use the same materials. For example, using red brick for pathways and construction if you have a red brick house will make the garden feel like an integral part of the whole property and give the sense that it has always been there. A whitewashed house will be beautifully offset by a whitewashed garden wall, and so on. Think, too, about colour themes you have used in the interior decoration and consider carrying them on into the garden. Try also echoing the shape of the building in some way. It is helpful, too, to consider the wider landscape – your neighbours' houses and the surrounding area. If you have a field to the rear, you can make a feature of it by framing your view with either plants or structures. If, on the other hand, your property backs on to the rear wall of somebody's garage or an industrial site, the view might be better off being concealed. You can 'borrow' the surrounding landscape or hide it with clever design. Always consider these options at the earliest stage.

Right: Here the imposing and complicated design detracts from the very plain wall behind. A busy backdrop would make this space feel claustrophobic.

THE PRACTICALITIES

If you're planning to undertake major work in the garden, access to a road is crucial, so you can remove unwanted materials from the site and bring in large deliveries. You may also need a skip, and it's essential that you have good access either so that the skip can be delivered or, if it's on the road throughout the project, that you are able to take the materials from your garden to the skip easily.

It's also vital to establish where the house services are – the depth and location of the mains electricity cables, phone lines and sewage, gas and water pipes – so you can work around them. The details are usually found on the plans to your house that were acquired when it was purchased, or your landlord should have them if you are renting. If there are no plans to your services or indeed they are inaccurate (as many can be if work has taken place without the changes being marked on a site map) then it is worth either having a little investigation yourself with extreme care and caution or even getting a surveyor in to assess your services. Regardless, it always pays to proceed with extreme caution when digging in soil, especially if you are making a fairly sizeable hole either for a tree or level change in the hard landscaping.

2. Size

It may sounds obvious, but the size of your garden will impact greatly on the sort of design you can realistically expect to achieve. In a large garden, grandiose schemes are more viable, but size brings its own problems – creating unity in a large garden can be tough and it may be worth considering breaking up the area into 'rooms' that are more manageable. A small garden obviously has limitations. These are usually of a practical nature; for example, you cannot always fit in everything you want. However, do not be downcast. It can be a wonderful opportunity to create all sorts of features that double up as something else. Benches with storage beneath them or seats that are also the edge of a raised bed or a low wall area are just a couple of clever ways to maximise your space. A small garden is also easier to design than a large one. The sooner you get your head around the space, both in terms of its limitations and potential, the more likely it is that you can arrive at a really practical design that suits your needs and makes the most of what you have.

Above: A small space can be immediately lifted with a whitewash to make it feel more roomy.

3. Levels

It may seem like a flat, level site is the easiest to design, and in some ways it can be. In reality, however, the most interesting designs incorporate some form of variation in level, although making alterations to the gradient of your land can be a costly business. A fire pit or sunken seating area will add interest, as well as some protection against wind if your garden suffers from the elements. If you have a slope already, think about ways of turning that into a feature. The cheapest way is to plant it, as the roots will stabilise a bank fairly quickly. Another way is to terrace it (using wood, brick or stone) then flatten off areas, rather like large steps. These flattened areas can then be paved or planted. Often, though, people feel the need to level off their garden, particularly if they like large areas of lawn. If a flat garden is something you really covet, you can level off a gentle slope with some re-landscaping – either by removing a large amount of earth or by introducing it. Make sure that you do not pile up too much (if any) directly against your house or overcompensate so that rain water runs towards the house, as this can cause problems with damp. If you are not fussed, I would recommend not messing about too much with the levels and instead consider working with what you have.

Below: Terracing can easily be turned into handy raised beds – great if you want to grow vegetables.

4. Shape

Just as the size of your garden will inform your design, so will the shape. A regular-shaped garden is fairly rare. They are more common in cities, but generally you will find irregularities and difficult areas. It needn't, however, be a limiting factor. An awkward shape can lend itself to features that actually make for a much more interesting design. One great way of combating an awkward shape is to use another within your design – a circle, for example, is a great shape for disguising problem areas.

Above: In a rectangular or square garden your design can be crucial in creating interest. Try breaking up the square with staggered pathways.

5. Drainage

This is the least glamorous part of garden planning. Drainage is inherently wet and muddy and can be soul destroying. There is only one thing worse than thinking about drainage and that is digging up plants that you've watched get less and less healthy, knocking down walls and pulling up paving because your garden is waterlogged. If you investigate the water situation before embarking on any construction you can install a drainage system in advance, which will mean you can grow a wider range of plants and have a much more pleasant and successful experience of building your garden. During all the aspects of planning and construction drainage should be at the forefront of your mind – then you can save yourself an awful lot of trouble.

6. Existing features

There is rarely a need to remove all existing features in a garden. Outbuildings or large, mature trees, for example, are expensive to remove and their presence can help to anchor a newly planted garden in its surroundings. Removing large existing features can also create unforeseen problems, such as exposing a view you didn't know was there or unearthing asbestos, rubble or large areas of concrete, the removal of which can put a project back and increase its cost quite considerably. It is amazing what a difference a coat of paint and bit of TLC will do to a tired-looking wall or shed. Consider these options carefully before making any drastic decisions that you might come to regret. If you decide to keep existing features, then it is worth repeating the materials elsewhere in the garden for a more cohesive look. This will also ensure that the features appear intentional and not like they have just been left there for convenience. Really consider them in the design so that they become a key part of your garden and not an afterthought.

Left: A mature tree gives the design more gravitas. There are some features that you can do nothing about, such as a telegraph pole, and these you will just have to learn to love.

7. Moisture levels

Annual rainfall averages for your area can be found easily online, but observations of your own garden are essential. For example, you may be in one of the driest parts of the country but a leaky drainpipe could mean that one small area of the garden is permanently moist. Alternatively, there could be a spring or stream nearby that causes the whole garden to be damper than expected. Conversely, large trees can be very thirsty and remove a lot of moisture from the soil, and if they have a dense canopy they can prevent rainfall from reaching the ground – particularly if the trees are evergreen – so even in damp areas you can have a fairly dry microclimate in your garden.

It's crucial to plant according to the soil's moisture level – moisture-loving plants in the dampest parts of the garden and drought-tolerant plants in the driest (see page 125). This has become particularly important in recent years, with more intense periods of drought and heavy rainfall, and the threat of hosepipe bans during the summer. Planting in the right place will reduce your water bills and save precious time, so you can sit and enjoy a glass of wine in the garden on a summer's evening, rather than walking around with a watering can in search of thirsty plants! **If you do ever have to water, make sure you water directly onto the soil, not the foliage, and give each plant a good long soak.**

VOLUME OF WATER TEST

If you are interested to know how much water your garden will receive throughout the year, place a few plastic bottles cut in half in different spots around the garden and measure the volume of water in them throughout the year. This will give you a very good idea of not only your rainfall, but where that rainfall actually reaches the ground.

8. Sun and shade

Note the direction your garden faces and how the sun tracks across it at different times of the day. You will discover the shady and sunny parts, as well as where you get the evening and morning sun – information that will help you plan your seating and storage areas as well as your choice of plants. It's best to monitor the tracking of the sun at different times of the year, as an area that's in full sun in the height of summer can be in shade in winter.

Some areas of the garden will be in permanent shade, such as those in the shadow of tall buildings, alongside the north side of walls, or beneath evergreen shrubs. In such situations, you'll need to select only shade-tolerant plants (see page 153).

The good news is plants that grow in the same conditions (whether sun or shade) naturally tend to look good together. So that takes care of your planting design.

9. Wind and shelter

If you live on a hill or by the coast, your garden is likely to be very windy. Town gardens can be surprisingly windy too, as wind can gust around the gaps between tall buildings in unexpected ways, making it stronger. Plants can suffer greatly at the hands of the wind: trees can rock and collapse if not planted to withstand the breeze, and leaves can suffer from wind scorch. In winter, wind chill can cause excessive damage when combined with already cold conditions.

You will probably find that your garden is either windy or it isn't. It is very difficult to determine exactly where the windiest spots are, especially with changing wind directions. However, it is the north-easterly winds that cause the most damage, so avoid putting your most fragile or tender plants in the path of these winds.

By adding a windbreak such as a wall, fence or thick hedge of tough evergreens, you can reduce the wind's strength considerably and provide some much-needed shelter in the garden, which will benefit you and your plants. That's why walled gardens were traditionally so popular as kitchen gardens – the wind was kept at bay, creating warmer temperatures that were ideal for ripening fruit and vegetables. I did my apprenticeship in a walled garden, and in some places in the garden you could feel only the tiniest breath of wind when a storm was gusting through. You will naturally find that the nearer the house you are, the warmer and less windy the garden will be.

Left: Although windbreaks are really a practical feature, there is no reason why they can't also enhance your design if used cleverly.

10. Hot and frosty spots

In summer there may be certain parts of the garden that become extremely hot. While it may be the ideal place for you to catch a few precious rays, many plants will struggle to grow in such situations. Similarly, during winter there will probably be particular spots that are more prone to frost than others. Or you may live in a 'frost pocket', which is a place that holds on to its frost for longer than other areas. Although these situations can be tricky for many plants, there is still a plethora of species that will thrive in them, so choose the right plants from the start (see page 125) and you will be rewarded in future years.

Above: Growing plants in containers means that you can easily move them out of extreme heat or cold as the seasons change.

LAVENDER

11. Soil type

Soils are made up of varying quantities of sand, silt and clay. Depending on where you live, your soil may also contain other materials such as chalk or peat that will affect its acidity. Climatic factors like rainfall and temperature will also affect the soil type you have, as will the amount of microbial organisms present in your area. All these elements and the quantities in which they are found in your soil (if at all) will affect the quality of your land and therefore have an impact on which plants will grow well in your garden. There are twelve main types of soil – mostly clay, mostly sand, mostly silt and nine other combinations of the three components. Nearly all soil types (the main exception being a waterlogged soil) can be improved with the addition of organic matter, such as well-rotted manure, but it's important to select plants that thrive in the particular type of soil you have in your garden (see page 125).

ROSES FOR RICH CLAY SOIL

SANDY SOIL

At the opposite end of the spectrum from clay, sandy soil is extremely free-draining and therefore by far the easiest type to dig as it's so light – the spade will cut it like a hot knife through butter. However, the disadvantage is that in summer you will be forever watering, and any nutrients you add to the soil will be washed or leached away very quickly. It can also be rather dry. Plants that tend to like sharp drainage, for instance many Mediterranean plants, such as lavender and *cistus*, tend to do well on sandy soil (see page 131).

SILTY SOIL

Sometimes called 'loam', this is often thought of as being the best soil type. It is free-draining yet water-retentive and naturally fertile – the magic combination as far as plants go. Most plants, even fussy ones, tend to do well on a silty soil. It is easy to dig so can be improved with the annual addition of some organic matter. This can be laid on the surface or dug in.

If you find your plants are getting too wet (as silt tends to occur in areas of wet or former wetland) then dig in some washed sand or grit to improve the drainage.

CLAY SOIL

If I had £1 for every time I heard a gardener complain about their clay soil I would be a rich woman! Certainly, it can be highly challenging. Clay soil is very moisture retentive, and therefore heavy and prone to waterlogging. When wet it sticks together so strongly that it makes digging nothing less than backbreaking, and when dry it bakes solid so it can be like smashing up concrete! However, on the plus side the propensity for a clay soil to hold onto water means that it retains nutrients, so it tends to be very fertile. Many plants, including roses, seem to prefer it to other soils (see page 139).

IDENTIFY YOUR SOIL TYPE

To find out what type of soil you have, wet a ball of soil about 5cm (2in) in diameter and follow this simple key:

- If the soil will not roll into a smooth ball it is sandy.
- Roll the ball into a flat sausage shape and bring the ends together to form a ring. If the soil splits it is silty and if not, it is clay.

12. Soil pH

Before planting anything in your garden, you will need to identify the acidity or alkalinity of the soil. This is assessed on a scale known as pH, with pH1 being extremely acidic and pH14 very alkaline. Most garden soils are in the middle of the range, or in Britain slightly on the acidic side of the spectrum, which suits most plants. Your soil type will be affected by where you live. For instance, you're likely to have a more alkaline soil if you live on down land, where the land around you is chalky, and in coastal regions, where there are high levels of salt in the atmosphere. On heath or moor land, your soil will most likely be very acidic.

There are various simple and inexpensive tests you can carry out to test your soil pH (see box, opposite). It is always worth testing in more than one area of the garden, particularly if you have a large plot. Test in open, exposed areas as well as more covered sites, as these may well differ; for example, areas under trees are likely to be more acidic, because leaf litter builds up and breaks down, releasing amino acids into the soil.

HOSTA FOR SHADE

PLANTS WHICH THRIVE ON ACID SOILS

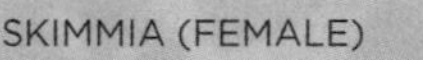

SKIMMIA (FEMALE)

RHODODENDRON 'CHRISTOPHER WREN'

ACER

TEST YOUR SOIL PH

You can test your soil using a simple testing kit from the garden centre. These kits are inexpensive, easy to use and accurate enough for the average gardener. Some use a probe that gives a pH reading, others use a solution that changes colour, with the shade indicating the level of acidity or alkalinity.

The old-fashioned way of testing pH is to use the vinegar and bicarbonate of soda method. This will not give you an accurate reading, but it will tell you whether your soil is acidic, alkaline or neutral. Fill a container such as an old ice-cream carton with a good handful of soil and pour in a few tablespoons of vinegar. If the soil fizzes a little, you have a slightly alkaline soil. If nothing happens, get another container full of soil and mix it with bottled water until the soil has turned to a sludgy liquid. Pour over a few teaspoons full of bicarbonate of soda. If this fizzes slightly, you have an acidic soil. If neither method produces any reaction, you have a fairly neutral soil.

SEDUM (ICE PLANT)

GRAPEVINE (VITIS)

...AND PLANTS WHICH THRIVE ON ALKALINE SOILS

RED HOT POKER (KNIPHOFIA)

IDENTIFY YOUR NEEDS

The next step in planning your outdoor space is to know what you want from it. This may seem obvious, but it's remarkable how often a garden owner overlooks his or her own requirements. It's also very subjective – a successful design to one person may be a nightmare to another.

You may be the type who will walk into a property, see an outdoor area attached to it, and rejoice at the thought of rolling up your sleeves, plunging your hands into the soil and having lots of plants to look after. Alternatively, your heart may sink at the prospect of the workload that lies ahead of you.

When designing a garden for a client, I always take the time to sit with a cup of tea and talk to them about their lives – their friends and family, hobbies and interests, and work routines – in order to decide how much time they will be able to give to maintaining their outdoor space, or whether they'd rather not put any time in at all. The key thing to remember is that the garden is your space, so create a design that suits your individual tastes, needs and lifestyle, and make sure you'll be able to maintain it easily. For garden enthusiasts, the ideal garden may involve growing plenty of flowers (including annuals) and having a pristine lawn and neatly clipped hedges. But this style of garden does not suit everyone. For those with a demanding full-time job, the responsibilities of a family, a busy social life, a tendency to travel, destructive pets and – perhaps most importantly – a lack of enthusiasm for garden maintenance, this style of garden would be incredibly difficult to keep on top of. In these circumstances, coming up with a design that will require less work will be far more compatible with your lifestyle. To help you decide on your priorities, work through the Questionnaire opposite.

QUESTIONNAIRE

Below are some questions to ask yourself before you design your garden. They should help you focus on your priorities and lifestyle, and come up with a garden to suit your requirements. Be as honest with yourself as you possibly can – about what you have time for and can afford, as well as your capabilities.

- Why do you want a garden? Are you interested in plants and look forward to tending them, or do you really just want an outdoor 'room' for relaxing and socialising?

- How much time will you realistically be able to dedicate to garden maintenance? Do you work full time or go away frequently? If so, consider selecting easy-care plants rather than fussy ones that require regular attention, and dedicate a large area to hard surfaces.

- Do you like to eat and entertain outdoors? If so, how many people do you entertain on a regular basis? Remember, you'll need to include a level area that is large enough to accommodate a suitably sized table and a sufficient number of chairs comfortably.

- Have you thought about including a second seating area, where you can enjoy the evening sun perhaps, or sit and reflect?

- Would you like to include a lawn? If you want a perfect green sward, do you have time to maintain it? Or are you relaxed about a few daisies, weeds and some moss?

- Would you like to include a water feature, such as a pond? (See page 78.)

- Do you plan to cook outdoors? If so, have you considered including an area for a barbecue in your design?

- Consider your storage requirements – will you need to erect a large shed for tools, garden furniture, bicycles and any overflow from the house?

- Do you need to include an area for hanging up washing? Would you like it to be in a hidden area of the garden?

- Do you want to grow fruit and veg? If so, would you like an area dedicated to them? Or just grow them in pots or in the flowerbeds with other plants? (See pages 166–183.)

- Are you interested in creating a garden that encourages wildlife, such as bees and butterflies? (See page 42.)

- Are children a consideration? For instance, will you need to include space for a swing, climbing frame or trampoline, or an area of lawn wide enough for a goal? Would the kids enjoy a small wildlife area or space for growing vegetables?

- Do you have pets? If so, are the boundaries safe to keep them in your and out of neighbours' gardens? You may choose to have areas of bare soil at the rear of borders to prevent pets from running on or making a mess in the flowerbeds or on the lawn. You may also need to include an area for hutches, runs or kennels.

- Do you need to accommodate someone with a disability? If so, you may need to create wide, safe, smooth pathways, gradual slopes rather than steps, and a seating area that will accommodate a wheelchair. Raised beds are good for disabled gardeners, as they are easier to maintain than beds at ground level.

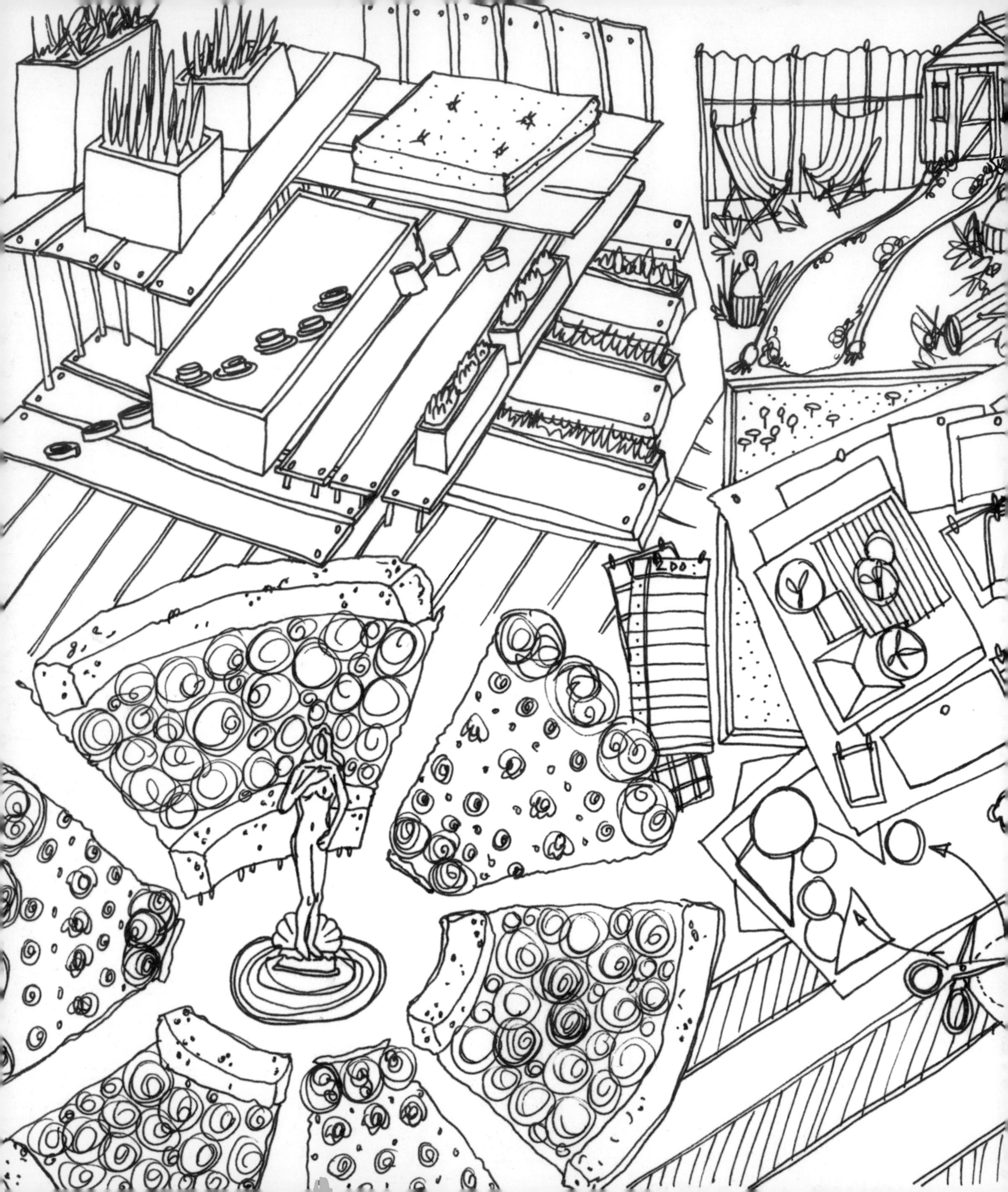
2DO

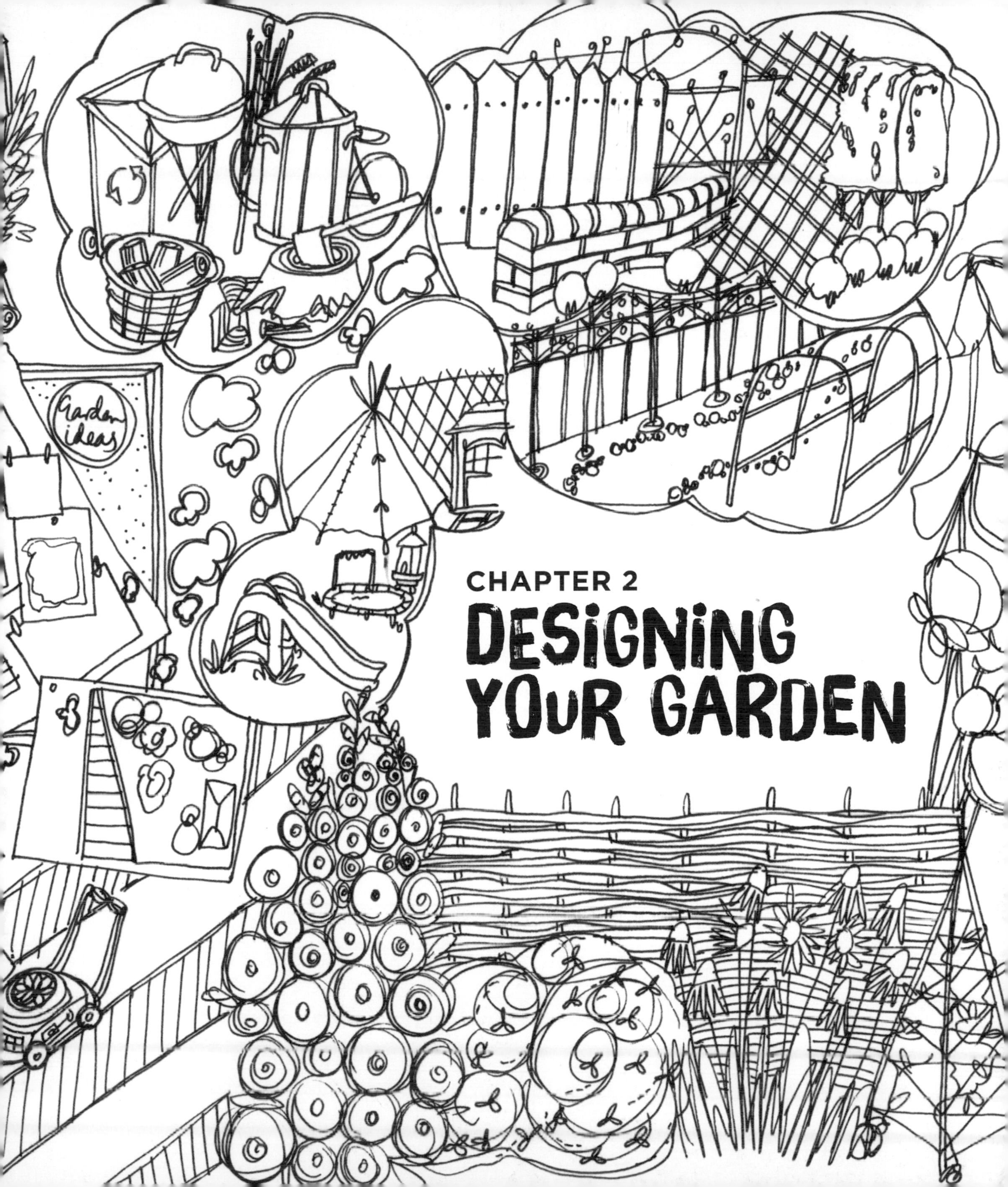

CHAPTER 2
DESIGNING YOUR GARDEN

THINKING ABOUT DESIGN

After carrying out your site survey and identifying your needs, you'll have a fairly good understanding of what type of garden you have and want to create. Now you need to work out what it's going to look like and where all the elements should go.

When you have little or no experience, designing a garden can seem a daunting task. However, the design process can be one of the most exciting and enjoyable aspects of creating a garden. If you take the time to really think the design through, it will pay dividends when it comes to the construction process, and you're more likely to be satisfied with your garden once it's finished.

Try to keep things simple and achievable: if you embark on the process with the intention of creating a finished garden à la *Grand Designs*, you'll only be disappointed. The key to enjoying this step and completing it successfully, without tears of frustration, is not to think of it as a garden design at all. Instead, just aim to create a pleasing 'picture'.

Throughout the design process, there are two words that should always be at the forefront of your mind – 'function' and 'form'. You're aiming to create a garden that is both usable and looks good aesthetically. Always consider the practical elements, and how they can be designed into the overall scheme in the most visually dynamic way.

If your budget allows, it can be helpful to call in a professional designer for either a consultation or to come up with a design for you.

GEOMETRIC CLIPPED BOX

1. Scale

Considering scale is essential when thinking about design. When you first draw up your plans it is crucial that they are to scale in order to guarantee a successful design. Features, unless they are bespoke, tend to come in fixed dimensions, so understanding your garden's scale will mean you eliminate the risk of wasting your money on structures that are either too small for the space or, worse, too big to fit! That's the technical element of scale, but there is also another, less tangible aspect, which concerns itself with how those features will look in the finished space in terms of their size. And it by no means follows that a small garden must only contain small features. More important is getting the balance of small and large features right. Big features in any sized garden often make a bold statement. The key here is really thinking about your scale, both with construction and in terms of planting. Play with scale, if you like, in order to create certain effects. A small bench, for example, is often used to make a space feel bigger. Remember that taller and wider structures are impactful but can be imposing, whereas smaller and narrower structures are more comfortable, less intimidating, but also easily overlooked. Crucially, make sure every decision is a conscious one and don't leave anything to chance.

A large container or urn makes a great feature (above).

2. Balance

This is a key part of any design, not just for gardens. To introduce balance is to create harmony. There are two kinds of balance in design; both create a more restful visual effect. First is to balance the whole space by repeating themes of colour, shape and size throughout the whole area. Using symmetry, especially on a diagonal axis, is a very easy way of doing this. Second is to balance individual features with something contrasting so that no one thing can be too dominant. For example, you can create a balance in scale by not letting one feature dominate. Another juxtaposed feature of large size somewhere else in the garden will counteract that dominance but so will the inclusion of smaller features around that large feature. Colour must also be balanced. Repeating a particular colour throughout a space creates a more harmonious design as does the inclusion of varying shades to either enhance or reduce the intensity of that colour depending on your colour scheme. Also think about balancing shapes. Spikes, circles and geometric shapes, such as squares and triangles, make a striking impact but creating balance from repeating the shape throughout the space or using contrasting shapes in conjunction with the original, takes the design to the next level.

Tall trees are balanced by planting at the base; here the purple sedum balances the greens (right).

3. Unity

Unity is the method by which you create a sense of cohesion or 'oneness' in a space. It might be achieved through repetition of a theme or colour or by using one key feature to tie the whole thing together. Something like a choice of paving stone used throughout the space might achieve this in a garden setting. Overlapping your shapes when creating the initial design will help create a natural unity. Using shapes of the same type for all your features will also help with this. Designs that feel bitty will do so because there is no unity. The design may have different components, such as a shed, a path or a flowerbed, but essentially they are all part of the same thing; the garden. Unity in your design will draw all those different components together.

Repetition of lavender and using the same stone for each pathway makes this space feel unified.

4. Proportion

Not to be confused with scale, which is much more technical and relates to individual features fitting in the space, proportion is all about relationships between features. Specifically this refers to their size. This covers the relationship objects and features have to each other as well as to the garden as a whole and even to neighbouring gardens and your house. To get the proportions right means that the garden will sit happily in its space. Garden features, when thinking about proportion, become parts of a whole – the whole being both the garden and also the street/area you live in. Again, this does not mean that a small space can only contain small features, but just that no one feature is allowed to dominate but is balanced by smaller features and also that the garden as a whole is not allowed to dominate too much over the house or neighbourhood. Everything should be in proportion with its surroundings.

Here the oversized water feature and diminished figure play with the proportions, creating a magical effect.

5. Texture

Texture is usually only skin deep insomuch as the surface is usually what gives something texture. With plants that is not always the case as foliage adds a huge amount of texture and is very three-dimensional. However, actively think about the texture of every material and feature and use it to really enhance your design. Smoothed stone next to fluffy foliage or rough wood next to metal are two examples of contrasting textures that give a sensory kind of interest to the space. All of these elements make for a well thought out design. One thing to beware of when trying to vary your textures is overcomplicating things. Think about unity and balance. Repeat materials and create unity and cohesion by having one material or plant or texture that holds all the others together.

Here the rusty metal creates a contrasting texture next to the plants, but the pink flowers echo the colour of the rust, bringing the design together.

6. Form

Form refers to the shape of individual features. Like texture, the most effective designs use varying forms cleverly to strike an interesting balance. If you look at a feature or a plant with your eyes half closed it becomes easier to see the shape rather than getting distracted by the finer detail. Use one form in different sizes for an impactful yet balanced design and vary it for something more restful. Use circles, mounds, curves and ovals for a soft look and spikes, spires, squares, triangles and straight lines for something more clean cut. Often, a combination of hard and soft forms works the best.

The circle is clean and offset perfectly by the upright linear forms of the plinth and plants.

7. Rhythm

Rhythm is created in a garden by using varying form, texture, colour and scale to create accents throughout the space. As humans we naturally find rhythm in all things. A regular rhythm gives us comfort subconsciously whereas irregularities unsettle us. The key with rhythm is the element of surprise. A totally regular and predictable rhythm is often dull. To throw in an unexpected accent every now and again keeps us interested, both orally and visually. If you have space to play with then try incorporating a change in rhythm in different areas. This can be achieved by having accents in colour or height, more or less frequently.

In this riotous border accents are created by injections of deep red against the otherwise green plants.

8. Perspective

This is something you will get anyway in your garden as it is inherent in a three-dimensional space. But using perspective to enhance your design is a very effective way of controlling how your garden looks. Very few of us have a perfectly square garden. Realistically, there will be irregularities in the shape. It may be that one side is longer than the other or that the space is much longer than it is wide or much wider than it is long. By using perspective you can create the illusion of length or width. Perspective is, in essence, the way things seem to diminish in size as they get further away. Making things actually diminish in size as they get further away creates the impression of length. Choosing bigger things for the end of the space will make it seem shorter and breaking up the space with physical barriers bamboozles the eye, meaning that you obscure the view and either break the space into smaller compartments or create the impression of something else beyond, which may or may not be there.

This small stone bench at the end of a straight pathway highlights perspective and makes the space look bigger.

9. Contrast

Contrast is very effective in design. By contrasting or juxtaposing different aspects of the design, you highlight the existing ones. A comfortable contrast is not too extreme, for example a circle next to a cone. These two shapes contrast each other but both have a curved element, though one also contains a straight line. A circle next to a square, on the other hand, would create an uncomfortable contrast because they are so vastly different. The trick is to use contrast subtly.

The smooth wood is contrasted by the fluffy box and spears of phormium. The foliage is contrasted by the metal birdbath. All these contrasts perfectly offset one another.

10. Concealing and highlighting

Concealing is a trick that is well worth perfecting in gardening as all gardens contain some features that may not be the most aesthetically dynamic. The water butt is a classic example. Compost bins and sheds can also be problem areas. Easier than turning these spaces into things of beauty, is to cleverly conceal or obscure them. This can be done with planting, with features, with a lick of paint or by using other areas to distract the eye away from these unsightly objects. On the other hand you might want to highlight certain features or areas. This can be done by putting them in a central position or by using plants and features to draw the eye towards rather than away from the object.

Here the trampoline has been cleverly obscured by the tall grasses (*miscanthus*).

11. Lines and curves

Lines and curves will happen anyway in the garden. Hard landscape features are more commonly straight as straight lines are easier to manufacture using hard materials. There is nothing wrong with straight lines; in fact, they are often easier to use to good effect than curves. But do take the time to consider your lines. A curved path can create a natural obstruction to the view that can be used to greatly improve either the look or function of a space. On the other hand a straight line can draw the eye around the garden. Do not underestimate the importance of lines and the effect they will have on your finished design.

Lay down a hosepipe or rope to mark out your curved pathways and create a natural shape.

12. Movement and flow

This is a hugely important consideration when designing your garden. It becomes even more significant when trying to create an effective design in an awkwardly shaped space. The flow of the space refers to how well one area merges into another. In a badly designed garden that flow will seem unnatural and forced. If you have good flow, you will probably find that you haven't noticed the transition until after it has happened. Movement refers to your movement around the space you have created. When considering this, put your practical head on. If you want to harvest vegetables to use for cooking, chances are you will want a fairly direct route from your vegetable patch to your kitchen. Traditionally veg patches are at the far end of the garden so you will either have to incorporate a straight-ish path to the end from your back door or move the vegetable patch so that it is nearer the house.

Desire lines are routes that you naturally want to take. Gardeners try to predict these lines and turn them into paths as they find that people will walk in that direction despite there being a flowerbed in the way. Try to do the same and create pathways in your garden that allow you to move all the way through the garden and use all the space. This does not mean putting a convoluted zigzag through the space, but creating interlocking pathways and features in areas that might otherwise be unused. The rotunda is a great tool; it was invented for areas that shoot off to one side or are triangular and is basically a paved circle, which may have a pond or seating area in it. From that circle a number of paths lead off in different directions. This allows you to maximise your use of the space. One final thing to remember is that pathways do not necessarily have to go from the house to the back. Diagonal paths are great for leaving the visitor guessing what comes next. And for a wide but short garden why not try flipping the whole thing 90 degrees and have the path running parallel with the house?

13. Focal points

Every space will have points that you want to make a feature out of. You may have sculptures or favourite plants that you want to really show off. If that is the case then turning them into a focal point is an incredibly effective tool. It also makes the visitor to the garden feel like they are being taken on a journey that's worthwhile. A focal point acts as a reward to the viewer. When they have walked down this path or that only to find that they are met with a dead end it can feel unsatisfying. To look left and see a sculpture or huge pot at the end of a pathway or avenue is somehow enriching and rewarding. Straight lines either created by plants, walls or pathways lead the eye and if you're going to lead the eye then there may as well be something worth seeing at the end of it.
If you have a focal point make sure its surroundings really show it off by accentuating the colour and shape.

GARDEN STYLES

When designing a garden, it helps to have a style, or 'look', in mind. Think about different garden styles, and what appeals to you. Some of the styles suggested here are traditional, but you can give any of them a modern twist if you like.

1. Cottage garden

The original cottage gardens were created to provide as much produce for the household as possible, with wildflowers and perennials used to fill the gaps between edible plants. Today, the term is used more loosely to describe a garden that is traditional and informal, with flowerbeds filled with flowering and edible plants all growing together in a seemingly ad hoc way. Cottage gardens are usually associated with 'old-fashioned' flowers, particularly perennials and self-sowing annuals, and traditional materials, such as local stone, old brick and timber.
For a modern twist, use straight pathways and clean lines.

2. Formal garden

Gardens that are formal tend to have a geometric, symmetrical layout, with straight lines and right-angled corners. Key features in traditional formal gardens include clipped evergreen hedging, paths (usually paved or brick) and planters. Formal gardens can be either traditional or modern in style.
For formal/traditional think Italian Renaissance.
For modern think clean/crisp and reduce the palette.

3. Contemporary garden

A contemporary garden is minimalist, light and clutter-free. It consists of clean lines and a large amount of hard landscaping. Plants are architectural, with distinctive, strong shapes (for instance spiky foliage or grasses). Stylish containers and creative lighting add to the modern feel.
To soften this style, use ground cover plants or mounding plants that obscure hard edges without creating fuss.

4. Wildlife garden

A garden that is created to encourage wildlife is filled with many colourful flowering and berrying plants to attract bees and birds. Plants with scented and single flowers are best.

In addition, you'll need to include piles of dead wood to provide insect homes during winter, trees and hedges for nesting birds, and a lawn for worms. You may also consider creating a pond (see page 78), which will attract breeding frogs, birds, small mammals and insects, such as dragonflies. Try to create a rich and diverse habitat – provide areas of shade as well as sunny, open spaces, and wet and dry areas.

Do not use chemical feeds or pesticides if you want to encourage wildlife and it is best not to have this style of garden if you own a cat or dog.

There is a misconception that wildlife-friendly gardens have to be messy and unruly, but this is not the case. You can design the space in any style you like; you can have a contemporary-style garden with straight, bold lines if you wish, and as long as you include the right plants and follow the guidelines above, you will certainly attract wildlife.

Painting wildlife-friendly features is a great way of modernising the look (below).

5. Themed garden

You may decide that your design will have a theme. It could be anything from the seaside with ropes, lobster pots, shells and pebbles to Italian-style with cypress trees, formal hedging and statues. Create a tropical paradise with big colourful flowers and huge leaves and hammocks or a fairy glen with small deciduous trees and dark, magical corners. A prehistoric, Jurassic theme could contain tree ferns and huge-leaved species or you might want to use white stone, clean lines and opulence to create something that evokes the feel of Monte Carlo, or even shiny metal and space-age furniture to produce something futuristic. Rusted metal and sparse planting might give a dystopian atmosphere. In other words, choose absolutely anything you fancy and think up a way to incorporate that theme into the design. Be as mad as you like, then rein in your most crazy ideas and think about a way in which they can be made practical or achievable.

Remember this is your garden. Make sure it expresses your personality.

HARD AND SOFT LANDSCAPING

Generally, a garden has two components: the hard landscaping and the soft landscaping. Hard landscaping (see pages 50–83) refers to all the surfaces plus any garden structures, barriers and water features. Soft landscaping means the plants (see pages 112–163). When designing and constructing a garden, you always start with the hard landscaping, because it provides the framework and because the planting is more flexible than the built elements; plants are easy to move around, while hard landscaping is not. Once installed, the hard landscaping is there for the long haul.

It can seem a bit nerve-wracking to start with the hard landscaping, but actually it's less difficult to plan than the planting. This is because when designing the latter you have to think about how the plants will grow and develop through the season and year after year, altering the garden scene, whereas hard landscaping stays put. In that sense, if you've never designed a garden before, starting with the hard landscaping will ease you in relatively gently.

SEEK INSPIRATION

Before you embark on your design, you may like to create a mood board. Take a large piece of card and stick down images that inspire you for whatever reason – perhaps photographs of gardens and garden features from magazines that appeal to you, or completely unrelated images such as those of buildings, cars, paintings, clothes, and so on. By collecting images that you feel are personal to you, you will start to see a pattern. It could be that certain colours, shapes or textures appeal, and you may discover you prefer smooth curves to geometrical angles, or vice versa. You can then bring these ideas into your garden design. Remember, designing is not about hard-and-fast rules but your own personal style and creativity.

MAKE A PLAN

First, you will need to draw an outline of your garden. This will need to be to scale. If you are lucky enough to have to-scale plans with the information you got when buying the house, then use those. Otherwise, you may need to measure the space.

Using metre-long lengths of cane is a really good way of measuring your plot. Otherwise get yourself a tape measure long enough for the purpose. Measure the length and width from different places as the garden may widen or narrow unexpectedly. Using satellite images online is a simple way of getting to grips with your garden's shape.

At this point it is also essential to think about the levels of your garden. If you have a slope then measure that, again with canes. How many metres in length does it take for your garden to drop its level by 1 metre? You will either correct this by excavating or bringing in more soil when the time comes, or you will work with the gradient by terracing. Either way, getting your head around your garden's topography and including it on your design is not just important, but imperative.

A scale ruler is a really helpful tool for drawing your garden accurately. You can choose the scale you use when drawing with it. Don't forget to include on your scale drawing any features that are already in the garden which you intend to keep. Try drawing on graph paper to help you really get your head around the dimensions and ensure accuracy. This can also help greatly when you're designing the features as the paper's squares can help you draw your design to scale. You can always trace the design in future to make the finished design look neater and easier to follow.

Once you have that drawing, make some copies of it and then just start playing with shapes. By that I mean draw out some shapes of differing sizes on a piece of paper and cut them out. Circles, squares and rectangles often work best, but if you have a plot of land that is an awkward shape, you may find that triangles, parallelograms, pentagons, rhombuses and hexagons work well, too.

Now you can start playing with the shapes by moving them around on the outline of the garden. It always makes a design feel cohesive if these shapes overlap to some extent. At this point, these shapes are shapes and nothing more. But once you start to have a pattern that you feel works quite nicely, you can start to think about what the individual shapes will become. For example, they could be pathways, sheds, arbours, patios, lawns or flowerbeds. If you're a confident draughtsman, you may want to just draw different shapes straight onto your plan.

Once you've done this, adding in all the features you would like to include and settling on a pattern that you find visually pleasing, start to think about how those features are going to fit into the shapes you have drawn. Really think about all the different elements of the design and how to make the space as practical and visual as you possibly can. (You may want to refer back to the questionnaire you did on page 23.) Also consider levels at this point – either working with existing level changes or introducing features like raised beds to create visual interest with changing levels. Mark all of these thoughts clearly on the design to save confusion in the construction.

Really go into specifics as well. Think not only about changes in levels, but also about how much those levels are going to change by – 'step of 180mm' for example rather than just 'step'. Think about edges, too; you will need to take these into account. Where one feature ends and another begins, for example with a raised bed going into the lawn, there will need to be a hard material creating that boundary. That will either shave a bit off your lawn or off your flowerbed. Really think about all of these components now to save yourself a headache later on. Once you feel you have a plan that you are really happy with, it's time to move on to the next step of the design...

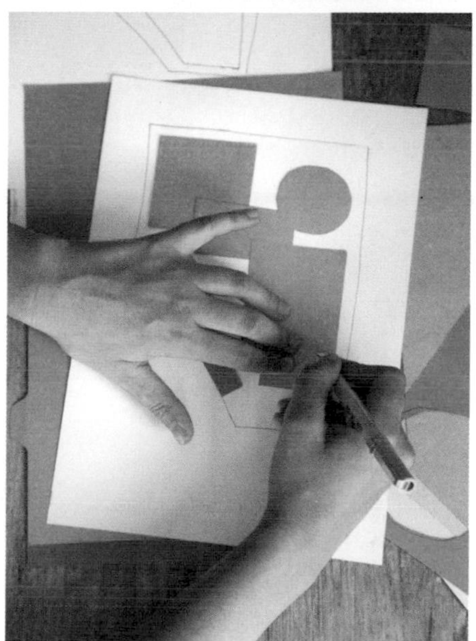

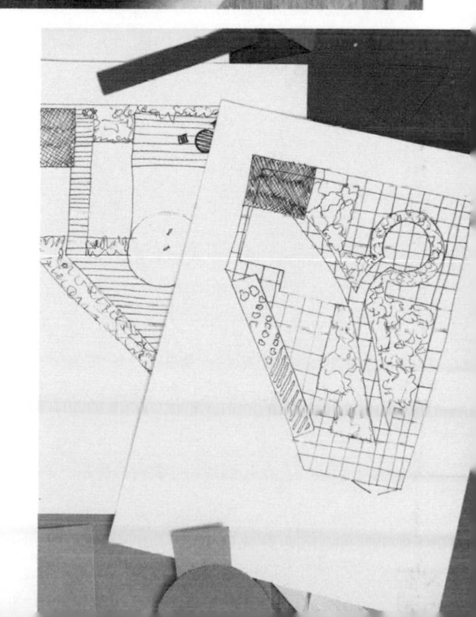

DESIGN CHECKLIST

The following list will prompt you to consider the different elements you might want to include in your garden design.

SURFACES

Paving (see page 64)
Gravel (see page 66)
Decking (see page 68)
Grass/lawn (see page 70)
Paths
Flowerbeds

STRUCTURES/BUILDINGS

Greenhouse (see page 82)
Conservatory
Summerhouse (see page 82)

BOUNDARIES AND DIVIDERS

Walls (see page 59)
Trellis
Screens
Hedging (see pages 132–136)
Espalier
Fencing and gates (see page 63)

UTILITY AREAS

Shed (see page 81)
Compost (see page 81)
Dustbins
Washing line
Kennel, hutch, coop or pen

DECORATIVE FEATURES

Pergola (see page 77)
Arbour
Arch (see page 77)
Wigwams
Gazebo
Planters
Statues
Lighting

CHANGING LEVELS

Steps (see page 75)
Terraces (see page 75)
Ramps (see page 75)
Raised beds (see page 75)

RECREATIONAL AREAS

Play equipment (trampoline, climbing frame, swings, paddling pool)
Sandpit
Barbecue

FIDO

CHAPTER 3

HARD LANDSCAPING

'Hard landscaping' refers to all the non-plant-related features, including paving, gravel, walls, fences, buildings, decorative structures and water features. These elements serve a practical purpose, but they're also extremely important in the overall design, as their shapes, positioning, and the materials from which they're created provide permanent structure, pattern, colour and texture. Hard landscaping can also be used to improve your garden layout. With clever planning, a patio, path or pergola can disguise an awkwardly shaped garden, provide interest in a basic rectangular plot, increase the feeling of space in a small area, and make a design more cohesive.

POSITIONING THE HARD LANDSCAPING

When planning hard landscaping, think through the final positions of features very carefully, as they will be difficult to move later. Think practically and try to foresee potential problems so you can avoid them.

The hard landscaping in your garden will create its permanent and immediate structure so really make a statement with it. Small structures will be lost where big ones will look great and hold the space together.

WHAT MAKES A SUCCESSFUL HARD LANDSCAPE DESIGN?

MAKE IT PRACTICAL

Don't design anything too ambitious and overcomplicated. Make sure everything you have included is either well within your own capabilities or you can afford to pay someone else to build it.

MAKE IT FUNCTIONAL

Position all the elements logically in the layout: a patio and play area for young children near the house, and the utility areas (such as a compost heap and storage) towards the end of the garden (ideally out of sight).

MAKE IT BEAUTIFUL

Just because most of the hard landscape features will serve a practical purpose, it doesn't mean you have to compromise on beauty. Make them reflect your style, whatever that may be.

MATERIALS FOR HARD LANDSCAPING

There is a bewildering array of hard landscaping materials available, including natural and man-made options. The materials you choose need to be practical, but ideally they will also be stylish and in keeping with the feel you want to create in your garden. Don't be afraid to have fun when thinking about materials – if you want to push the boundaries of normality, do so!

Cost may well be an important consideration, particularly as the hard landscaping is usually the most expensive aspect of creating a new garden and any new homeowner will have just spent a lot of money on fees and deposits and may not have much left over. However, think creatively and it may not cost as much as you fear. For instance, you may find that in carrying out work in the house you have materials that have been ripped out of the interior. Rather than throwing them all into a skip, recycle them for outdoor use. You could turn an old cabinet into a planter by taking off the doors and turning it on its side or even use old copper pipes to keep the slugs at bay! Not only will you make savings, you'll end up with something bespoke and interesting rather than bought off the shelf. You can also make regular visits to scrap yards, salvage yards or even the local tip and scavenge for materials that can be used in the hard landscaping construction. Old cabinets, pallets, furniture or just scrap bits of timber can be turned into a plethora of things with a little imagination.

Railway sleepers are very popular for the construction of raised beds, terracing, steps, paths and edging and are extremely strong. They do come with a health warning, though. If you are buying old railway sleepers, try to avoid touching them with your bare skin, as some of the treatments they will have been given in their working life are likely to have been highly carcinogenic. So either wear gloves or give your hands a good wash after you touch them and especially before you eat. These substances are also highly toxic to plants, so if you're planning to turn your wall into a raised bed, staple or nail a butyl liner to the back surface of the sleeper (between the wood and the soil) to stop those chemicals seeping into the soil. Now really people should not sell you sleepers soaked in creosote, but a few may slip through the net, especially if you are buying them secondhand. A much better idea is to buy them new and therefore totally untreated. That saves all kinds of problems and is really the only thing that you should use if you can possibly help it – and is essential if you have children or pets.

If you're not comfortable with the idea of building your own garden structures, yet like the idea of a bespoke look, there's nothing to stop you buying pre-fabricated items from a garden centre or builders' merchants and clad them in more striking materials. At least you'll know they're structurally sound!

It's always useful to visit a garden centre or builders' merchants to get hands-on inspiration about these materials – how they feel and look and the size, weight and even the smell of them. You may be surprised how much these materials differ from their photographs.

BOUNDARIES AND DIVIDERS

Most gardens have some kind of boundary marker, such as a wall or fence, to delineate the perimeter of a site and separate you from your neighbours, discourage intruders and provide privacy. You might also want to divide up the garden internally – perhaps you want to keep children or pets out of certain areas, or you want to create visual interest and a sense of intimacy and enclosure.

The type of boundary you choose will probably depend on the purpose of the barrier, the look you want to create and your budget. Walls and heavy-duty fences are solid but expensive, and while they may be the best option for marking a boundary you might prefer to use a more ephemeral divider, such as a lightweight fence, trellis or screen. Bear in mind if you opt for a fence that ends up being too exposing that you can always grow plants to fill in the gaps and preserve your privacy. Hedges also make excellent boundaries and dividers and have various benefits (see pages 132–136).

Walls

There's a vast range of materials you can use for walls, including stone, brick, reconstituted stone and concrete blocks. Before building a wall, consider your location and the materials used for the house and surrounding buildings – it's best to create a unified look if you can.

STONE

Stone is a classic natural material that suits both modern and traditional styles of garden. There is a multitude of stone types available, in different colours, shapes, sizes and textures, so I suggest you go to your local builders' merchants and pick up a leaflet; try a few outlets to really establish your options.

It's always nice (though it can be a little pricey) to use a local stone for construction, although what you spend on local labour you often save on delivery costs. It varies according to region and in some areas, for example those with a chalky parent rock, you will find local stone is unsuitable for building. However, if you live in a sandstone, limestone or granite region then you will be very able to use the local stone. The advantage is that it ties the garden nicely into its surroundings, particularly in rural areas. It also saves the air miles on what are quite heavy goods.

You may find that certain stones are cheaper than others, especially some that are imported and don't have the associated costs of local labour or fair-trade restrictions. I would be tempted to spend a little more and buy something local, but if cost really is a constraint then raj stone is very popular. It is a form of sandstone imported from India with a warm or pinkish hue and some mottling. It is probably one of the cheapest options available but there are other, slightly more expensive, choices. York stone is ever popular and has a warm, golden colour. Quartzite is a very hard stone that comes in a range of colours, from pink/grey to deep grey/silver and a golden that's almost orange. Sandstone is a favourite for walling as it has a sedimentary form that makes it easy to quarry in straight blocks. As its name suggests, it is often a sandy colour. For a contemporary look, slate is popular. It is deep, dark grey, sometimes verging on purple or blue, and with small, thin, tile-like blocks it can make a bold statement.

Another thing to consider when ordering your stone is the sizing. Unlike brick, stone tends to come in slightly varying sizes. If you want a really modern finish you may have to pay more for stones that have been cut to an exact size. You can often roughly choose the block size but they will not be uniform. It's worth double-checking when you order that you are getting just what you want. Sometimes going to the supplier is the safest option and it's also worth asking if you can take a sample away with you. Any hard landscaping is not only a big investment, but is very hard to rearrange. It's worth taking the time to get these decisions right from the start.

In a traditional rural garden, a dry stone wall is hard to beat. Dry stone walling is a real skill, as each stone is balanced on the lower slab and no mortar is used, so unless you're an expert, you'll probably need to hire the services of a local specialist.

Alternatively, you will need to use concrete to hold your stones together. A quick cheat is to create the look of a dry stone wall by cementing stones together in the centre only, so the mortar is hidden from view, and leaving them unpointed. This will leave cracks and gaps in the face of the wall, which you can fill with plants as you would a 'proper' dry stone wall (see box, page 60).

Remember the rules of design when choosing hard landscape materials. A wall can be broken up with a contrasting form like this rustic container (below). Choosing similar materials for this and other features will create unity and avoid the problem of overcomplicating the look.

CAMPSIS – A CLIMBER

GROWING PLANTS IN WALLS

Some shallow-rooted plants that require very little soil look great growing in crevices of walls and can really bring such hard landscaping to life. Flowers such as *Erigeron* species, perennial wallflowers (*Erysimum*) and valerian, and some ferns, are just a few such plants. Choosing species of plant that naturally grow in walls also means that you will need hardly any compost at all for them. Even a little handful of topsoil from the garden put in the cracks will make a good home for a wall species. It couldn't be simpler; keep them watered initially but from then on the roots will scramble through the cracks with very little effort required from you. Cut them back a little if they are getting unruly, but even this should not be required much as many of these plants never get too leggy but just run along the cracks in little mounds.

BRICK

The most commonly used material for building walls, brick is a great way of visually unifying the house and the garden. Unlike stone, brick is not a naturally occurring material. It is basically baked earth – a little bit like pottery. There are different colours of brick depending on the earth that was used to create it. Red brick is most commonly used for landscaping, but yellow brick is also very attractive. You can buy new bricks from builders' merchants or secondhand from a reclamation centre if you want a mellower, aged finish. And because bricks are man-made it is also possible to get them in varying sizes. Small bricks give a slightly more intricate look. As well as this there is the option to use half bricks or even quarter bricks, so you really do have a lot of scope for variation.

And the options do not end there. There are all kinds of different styles of bricklaying. Every brick has the potential to be laid in one of six ways. There's the short face that can be visible either on its side (header) or on its end (rowlock), the long narrow face has the same two options (stretcher or soldier) as has the long, wide face (shiner and sailor). The most common style of brickwork is the Flemish bond, which alternates headers and stretchers. A monk bond uses the same style but rather than one stretcher between each header, it has two. The Sussex bond uses three stretchers. There are styles that alternate entire rows of either headers or stretchers and of course some styles that use just one face of the brick throughout the whole wall. There are also some more decorative styles, such as basket weave where pairs of shiners and sailors are laid alternately and herringbone style where bricks are laid on a diagonal, although this is much more commonly seen in paving.

It's important to ensure the bricks are frost resistant and suitable for hard landscaping, as not all bricks are. Some absorb too much moisture when in constant contact with damp soil, and as a result they become covered with moss or algae and crumble in frosty weather. For this reason it is worth putting copings on the tops of walls. A coping is a cap on the top of the wall designed to protect the bricks from rainwater that would otherwise sit on the surface of the wall and cause problems.

Bricklaying is a complex skill that takes time to learn, so it's best left to a professional. The key points to bear in mind are that a wall must be built on stable foundations, to eliminate any risk of movement, and once laid each brick must be level.

CONCRETE BLOCKS

Other man-made materials suitable for use in constructing walls are breeze-blocks and other cement-based options, although you may find they're less attractive in the garden than bricks or natural stone. However, they are useful if you're trying to create an edgy style, or you can render then paint them, which can be a really lovely look. White opens up a space and will make any garden feel fresh and bright and almost Mediterranean. Alternatively, for an even more exotic look, bright colours can make a really big impact and make the garden feel cheerful all year round. Another reason why this is so liberating is that breeze-blocks are quick, relatively easy and cheap to lay, which means you don't feel so nervous about covering them with paint. You can also change the colour every few years as part of a dramatic rejuvenation.

As the old saying goes, where there's a wall there's a gate (unless, of course, there isn't). But in all seriousness, unless the wall is there as an integral part of a terracing system, you will have to think about access and including gaps for gates in your design. It is not always necessary to make your gates in a straight line. In fact, staggering them slightly might encourage you to use more of your garden. Gates are usually made of wood but if you don't want to confuse your design by adding too many different materials then you can just leave a gap in the wall. I would not recommend doing this on a boundary wall, though, as this will encourage trespassers. A painted wall might be improved by a painted gate, either in a similar colour for something calming or in a contrasting colour for a more exciting finish.

Fences, trellis and screens

Timber is the most usual material for fences and trellis. It is relatively inexpensive, easy to cut and shape and reasonably long lasting if treated to protect it from the weather. Softwood timber (from conifers such as pine, cedar and larch) is the most common and least expensive option for external use. Hardwood (from broad-leaved trees such as oak, ash and chestnut) is longer lasting but more expensive and difficult to work with.

Pressure-treated timber for outdoor use is available from a wood yard. You can buy pre-fabricated panels, or planks of timber from which you can then construct your own fencing or trellis. Pre-fabricated panels are the least expensive option, but you may prefer bespoke fencing if your garden is an awkward shape, or if you want to make the design a little more unusual.

There are many different styles of fencing. Featherboard fencing is made from upright boards that have a slight overlap. Palisade or picket fencing is the typical cottage-garden fence made from uprights with pointed tops, which typically only comes up to waist height. One of the most common and inexpensive forms is the larchlap panel. This is a framework with horizontal planks attached. An interwoven fence is similar but the slats are woven rather than overlapped. Jacktop fencing is usually only half height and is a criss-cross style with the wood set diagonally. A wattle or hurdle fence is a very popular option, especially for those who want a more traditional and rustic look. Often made from hazel, usually with sweet chestnut uprights, this is a woven fence.

I would highly recommend having a fence or wall along the boundary of your land. However, there is nothing stopping you from also having some fencing throughout the garden itself. You may want to keep the children in or the pets out. An internal fence will be different in style from one along the boundary as there is no security issue

USING METAL IN THE GARDEN

Metal will almost always give you a modern, sleek effect, unless it is very rusty. If you don't like rust, choose either stainless steel or galvanised metal. Metal palisade fencing might give more of a feel of a railway line or an industrial depot than a garden. Alternatively, you can create a very modern fence by using metal uprights with strategically placed gaps between them. These gaps should obviously narrow enough so that nobody can fit between them or such fencing can be used within the garden to section or screen off areas. Hedging can be used in much the same way – with strategically placed gaps that give a contemporary twist to a traditional feature. You might even want to use a more traditional material such as timber or stone and then clad or partially clad it in metal. The same goes for any feature walls or raised bed walls. For a stylish finish, use brick, concrete blocks or wood clad with metal instead.

associated with it. You may find that you want the fence to be much lower as there is no need to maintain your privacy within your own space. By extension you may also want to consider having a fence that allows light through it. For this purpose something like a trellis might be just the ticket. You can think very differently about internal fences. Why not try creating something bespoke using recycled materials like glass bottles or driftwood? And there is always the option of using plants as a barrier. A screen of bamboo, for example, is evergreen, thick, sturdy and yet is ephemeral enough to allow the wind and light to pass through it. Screens or fences can be used to enhance your outdoor space visually as well as performing an essential and important practical task. So think about ways to exploit the aesthetic aspects of your chosen fencing material.

INSTALLING A FENCE

To install a wooden fence, you will need some hefty upright stakes as support. They can be brick or concrete, but pressure-treated softwood stakes are the easiest and least expensive option, and they will blend in seamlessly with the finished article. There are two ways to fit the uprights: either put the posts into a hole and fill the hole almost to the top with quick-setting concrete, or hammer special metal casings into the ground and then slot the posts into the casings. This is a good option for those who don't like long-term commitment as it gives you the chance to move things around fairly easily in the future should you change your mind. Once your posts are in, simply attach the fencing panels to them using screws.

Depending on the kind of fence you choose, the maintenance will vary, but all timber fencing will require some periodic TLC to keep it in peak condition. Most timber used for fencing will have been pressure treated. If you are making a fence from scratch then make sure you buy pressure-treated (or Tanalised) timber. This reduces the maintenance as the wood will be much more able to cope with the elements than an untreated alternative. However, that does not mean that treatment is not required. Your fences will have a much longer life if treated with an exterior wood paint or preservative. Regularly check the base of the fence as this is where there will be most contact with damp and rotting is most likely to occur. Check fence posts for any rotting because if one of these snaps you may find it bringing a large part of your fence down with it.

For hurdling fences the maintenance is a little more intensive. As with any fence made of thinner timber you may occasionally need to replace parts that have snapped in heavy wind. Hurdling is not pressure treated to preserve the wood as the bark is left on the branches. However, that bark will aid in preserving the timber. It is very rare to find painted hurdling as it does not look quite as nice and there is no real need for it as the bark protects the wood. This means that the maintenance can be more than an annual coat of paint and when repairs need to be made they can be extensive, sometimes requiring whole new panels.

Timber is a very profitable business worldwide and the illegal timber trade is incredibly difficult to police across borders where legislation and penalties vary so much. Certain species of timber are on an endangered list called SITES. If you ever see timber for sale that is on this list then avoid buying it. There are also plenty of timber products (both living and harvested) that are entirely legal but still unsustainable and involve deforestation of precious and ever-diminishing areas. If timber (or plant material) has been sourced sustainably there should be an FSC (Forestry Stewardship Council) label on the product. Look out for this and wherever possible try to only ever buy sustainable timber products.

The different fence options available will serve different functions but, crucially, will also have a very different look – some modern, some rustic, some vernacular. Choose carefully,

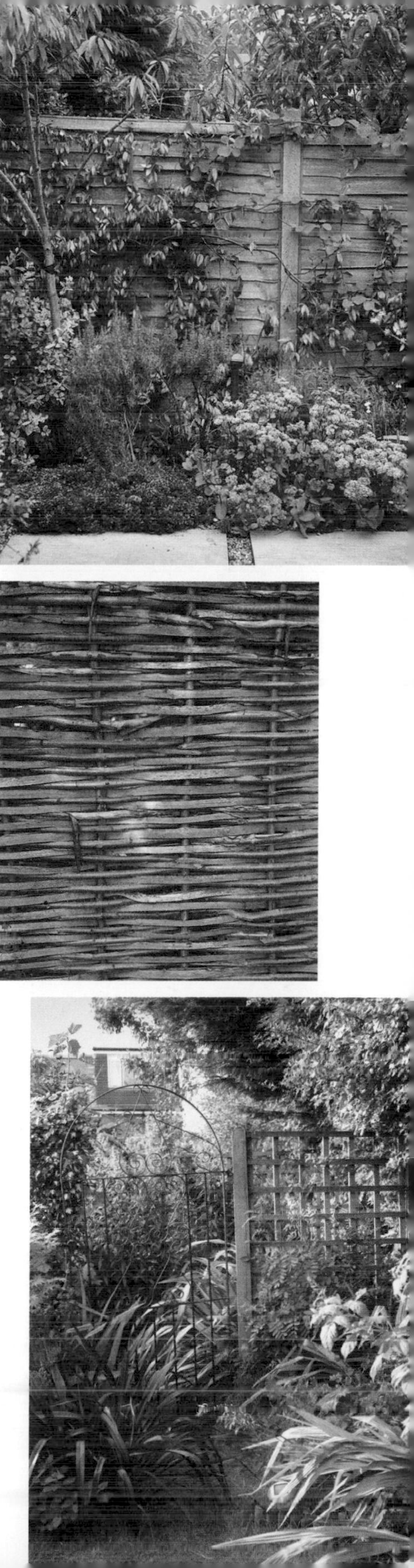

SURFACES UNDERFOOT

Paving

Paving, like walling, is entirely a matter of taste. Styles of paving range from the extremely traditional, such as cobbles or brickwork, through to the extremely contemporary, such as stone tiles or extensively smoothed stone. And just like choosing materials for walls, the cost can be hugely variable. In much the same way it pays dividends to think carefully about your choice of material. The vast range of stone available nowadays means that it is easy to choose a stone that will achieve the look you are aiming for in terms of style, while still being in keeping with the landscape surrounding your garden. Bricks of all different colours are available that will potentially match the brickwork of your house and sets (which are imitation bricks) are a cheaper option that allows you to choose even more varying colours and, crucially, sizes for your paving. Stone of all different colours can either be natural and random in size and shape, squared off but still with natural imperfections and lumps and bumps on the surfaces, or smoothed entirely for a look that's very simple and chic. As with walling, it is well worth making a trip to the stone merchants to look at and feel the stone and gauge the prices before making your final decision.

Also have a good think about the style of paving you are going to lay. It can be a nightmare to start a job, having ordered enough in metres squared, only to find that you have not thought at all about the laying pattern and you have to make awkward cuts in the slabs and may even find yourself short of stone in the end. Draw up the measurements of the area you wish to pave and make a scale drawing once you have decided on the paving and size of the slabs, bricks, sets or cobbles.

By all means visit a stockist to get ideas for paving styles, but for those on a budget, there may be the option to lift existing stones or bricks and re-lay them to your own design.

HOW TO ... LAY PAVING

- Dig out the soil to a depth of about 20cm (8in) and roughly level the surface.
- Add a layer of weed-suppressing membrane on top.
- Cover the membrane with a layer of MOT type 1 or sub-base (hardcore) to a depth of at least 10cm (4in). Make sure it is compacted and level.
- Add a layer of sharp sand or a sand and cement mix then a layer of sand. The total depth of these two layers should be 25–40mm. At this stage you might want to consider some haunching, which is an edging of cement that runs along the outer stones giving support to a paved area. This will stop stones from becoming loose over time.
- Place a paving slab on top, allowing a gap of 1cm (0.5in) between slabs. Gently tap it level using a rubber mallet. Check the paving is level using a spirit level. Repeat with the other slabs.
- After 24 hours, point the gaps between the slabs using the same cement mix or brush soft sand into the gaps.

To make a space look longer you may want to put the slabs in lines and align the gaps between the slabs, but generally the technique is to overlap the stones so that the gaps between two slabs are staggered from one row to the next rather than lining up. This makes for a stronger finish and is often visually more pleasing, although the choice is yours. Herringbone and basket weave brickwork are two stylistically interesting methods of brick paving but there are many others. One method popularised in the early 20th century when laying terracotta or slate tiles was to have them lying on their side so that only the thinnest edge shows on the surface. This is particularly handy for laying circles but will naturally use a lot more tiles than other methods.

With the range available on the market there is no reason why you can't have exactly what you want laid in exactly the way you like. So take the time to consider all your options.

Laying paving is really nothing to worry about, and once you get into your stride you'll wonder what all the fuss was about – trust me. Basically, all you're dealing with is a paving slab and a substance that will support it. For a really strong paved area that will not wobble or sink, use a semi-dry cement bed of three parts sharp sand to one part cement and a little water, to lay your paving on to. You can use sharp sand alone, but the paving is more likely to shift a little.

The main points to remember about paving are the levels and falls. Levels means each slab must sit level in the cement or sand. To achieve this, compact the layers of sub-base and sand or cement and use a spirit level to check the paving. The fall is how the overall paving slopes. Since paving cannot soak up rain like a lawn or flowerbed, it needs to be set on a slight slope to prevent water collecting on the surface. Make sure the paving slopes (or 'falls') away from the house, otherwise there may be puddling and damp patches collecting at the base of its walls. As a rule of thumb, aim for a slope of around 1 in 40 – that's a fall of about 2.5cm (1in) in every metre (40in) of length. In short, this is a very gradual slope downwards away from any building.

Gravel

A very popular option for surfacing, gravel is extremely easy to lay, inexpensive and versatile in terms of design. Its neat look suits a modern or traditional-style garden, it is ideal for large expanses or small areas (including tiny or awkward gaps) and adds definition without being harsh. It is also an environmentally friendly choice, as rainwater drains through it easily – unlike solid surfaces, which it runs off, sometimes causing flooding.

Gravel is available in a huge range of different sizes, colours, textures and materials, including flint, slate and glass. There is even self-binding gravel, which gradually compacts and resists movement as it's walked on, and resin-bound gravel, which will not move underfoot because it is suspended in a hard resin. (The latter two are more labour intensive to lay than other types of gravel.)

For extra stability on your gravelled areas, you can buy a honeycomb grid that goes beneath the gravel, holding the stones firmly in place.

LAYING & MAINTAINING GRAVEL

To lay ordinary gravel, all you have to do is dig about 10cm (4in) down into the soil, lay a weed-suppressing membrane, pour the gravel on the top of it until it is up to the same level as the surrounding areas and rake it until it's level. You'll also need to define the perimeter of the area to be surfaced with edging (such as bricks or kerbstones), to keep the gravel within bounds. If you are laying gravel for an area of hard standing, you will need a layer of compacted sub base about 10cm (4in) thick beneath the gravel.

The main disadvantage of gravel is that you will need to top it up periodically, as it becomes tired looking and diminished as a result of cars driving on it, people walking over it and inadvertently kicking it, and in some cases children digging it up and throwing it around. However, it's a small price to pay considering its benefits and the fact that it is quickly and easily refreshed.

Decking

Ah, the humble deck, so often associated with trips and slips, algae growing in the dampest corners, and the 1990s. But decking became as popular as it did for a reason. The colour and texture of wood sets off plants beautifully and creates a very natural look. Decking also retains heat more than paving, making it much more pleasant to step out onto. It's an extremely useful way to deal with awkward garden shapes and levels, as it allows for a more flexible design than paving, including curved shapes. Plus all those things we later found out about decking – how perilous it is in drizzle, or how prone it is to algae and rotting – no longer apply because technology has caught up so there are many more practical options than there used to be.

DECKING MATERIALS

If you're worried about a deck becoming slippery in the rain, you can try a composite deck made from recycled plastics. This will eliminate the slip risk and will not fade in colour as wooden decking does. Alternatively, you can get plastic decking with a thin veneer of a rubber-like material that is cast from real wood, so that it has a sort of railway sleeper or driftwood effect. It can look really effective and, again, will remain hazard-free in rain.

If slipping doesn't concern you, go for something wooden – and that doesn't necessarily mean the traditional pine options. Hardwood is particularly attractive, and with a stain of some kind, especially a high-gloss varnish, it can make your decking look more like the floor of the Ritz than a garden surface. Just make sure that the wood comes from sustainable sources (see page 63).

If you do go for a classic pine deck (and it will be the cheapest option), you may want to paint it an interesting colour. There is a wide range of exterior wood paints available, from the subdued hues of natural colours to fun and exotic brights.

Building your own deck is easier than you might think (see left). Keep it clean to prevent a build-up of algae, and treat it with exterior preservative every year or two.

A top tip for any budding hosts and hostesses is that decking is a very easy surface to incorporate lighting into.

HOW TO... BUILD A DECK

- Create a strong framework of vertical and horizontal supports using Tanalised or pressure-treated timber. This framework should fit snugly around the space you want to deck out.
- The whole structure then goes on the ground and is held in place by stakes that should already be cemented in place.
- Build the surface of the deck by attaching the planks with screws, ensuring that the gap between each is the same width – about 5mm will be sufficient to allow rainwater to drain through.
- Cut any awkward shapes using a saw. For a neat finish, think about cladding the edges and visible sides in the same material that you used for the deck. In order to do that, simply screw deck boards to the edge to cover the framework beneath. Make sure you sand the edges beforehand for an even more professional finish.

Lawns

Turf is a great asset in the garden and is very versatile; as such, it should not be underrated or snubbed in favour of hard surfaces. It provides a lovely soft place to sit, lie and walk on, and who can possibly resist the smell of cut grass on a summer's day? If you have children or pets, a lawn of some kind is almost essential. What's more, a lawn is more environmentally friendly than hard surfaces. It provides a habitat for numerous creatures, and helps to avoid the excessive flooding we've seen in recent years and are likely to see more of in years to come. This is because it allows rainwater to drain through, rather than sitting on the surface of tarmac or paving and having nowhere to go, resulting in it eventually streaming down the street and causing flash floods.

Maintaining a perfect lawn takes hard work, dedication and a little know-how, but the initial outlay for its creation is minimal. It is often thought of as a traditional feature, but if it's kept in good condition and grown in a considered shape it can be every bit as modern as an area of paving or decking – especially if used in conjunction with other hard landscaping materials. It is one of the only materials that can be used on a steep gradient or to cover land forms. Try using this for a contemporary style.

And whilst I am in the full throes of a crusade to fight the lawn's corner, I may as well talk about the other kinds of lawns – the less pristine ones, which are better for wildlife as chemicals aren't used to maintain them. Wildflower meadows are very in vogue at the moment. They are beautiful and very low maintenance, needing only two cuts per year. If you don't want to go the whole hog and plant a meadow in your garden, consider a chamomile lawn. It's a member of the daisy family that forms a lawn-like mat with small white flowers and a heady scent as it's crushed underfoot. Still not convinced? Then how about a normal, bog-standard lawn, not the pristine kind but the sort that's full of daisies, plantain and moss. Not hard work to maintain, like its purer cousin, but soft to walk on, good to look at and more wildlife-friendly.

ASTROTURF

If you like the look of a lawn but aren't able to keep up with the maintenance required, consider the option of artificial grass (astroturf). Personally, I don't quite understand the concept of plastic grass, but colleagues and friends who have used it tell me that it's great stuff, and that nowadays, with improved engineering, it really does look like the real thing. It is hardwearing and therefore particularly useful if you have someone in the family who enjoys ball sports or other games that would take their toll on a real lawn.

TYPES OF LAWN

There are various types of lawn seed mixtures available, so choose one that suits your garden and individual needs. First, consider the conditions in your garden. For instance, is it particularly shady, sunny, dry or damp? There are seed mixtures to suit all situations. Next, consider what you want the lawn for. Is it important for you to have a perfect sward to look at and admire (in which case you'll need a fine- or luxury-grade mix), or is it more essential to have a lawn that is hardwearing, tolerates neglect and can withstand heavy traffic, as needed in a family garden? If the latter, opt for a mix that contains ryegrass, as it will be more resilient and require less maintenance. If you want to create a wildflower meadow, you can buy a wildflower/grass mix. Some people prefer buying strips of ready-grown turf rather than sowing grass seed. This has the added advantage of seeing the turf before you buy it.

The great thing about a lawn is that it will fit into any shape of garden. Although a roll of turf comes in rectangular strips, with a half moon or edging iron, it can easily be cut into any shape you can think of. It can zigzag, wave or gently curve with the greatest of ease. A really good way to create a curve you are happy with is to use a rope or even a hosepipe and lay that down on the grass until you have the shape you want. Then spray that shape in place and cut. If it's straight lines that excite you then set up a string line for a perfect straight edge.

Every garden is a slightly different, irregular shape. To get a really good idea of the shape for lawns and other features, try viewing them from an upstairs window.

HOW TO... PREPARE THE SITE FOR A NEW LAWN

- Clear then dig over the site thoroughly.
- Rake the ground level and remove large surface stones, old roots and so on. Break up any big clumps of soil.
- When the soil is level, it's a good idea to add some grass fertiliser.
- Firm the soil by walking all over it to create a firm, level bed.
- Rake again to a fine tilth.

CREATING A NEW LAWN

If you decide to lay a lawn, you have two options available. The least expensive but slowest method is to scatter grass seed. Alternatively, if you haven't got the time or patience for that, you can lay pre-grown turf to give you an instant lawn that can be enjoyed almost straightaway. Whichever type of lawn you choose, remember it's best to position it in an open site that gets sun for much of the day, so avoid shady areas and overhanging trees.

Whether you're sowing seed or laying turf, you'll need to prepare the site for your new lawn in the same way before you start (see page 71).

HOW TO SOW SEED

First, prepare the site as described on page 71. Sow the seed straight onto the soil in late summer or early autumn, when there is sufficient rain and weeds are not at their most fiercely competitive. Alternatively, you can sow it in early spring if the weather isn't very cold or dry. You can protect the seed from birds with netting, though this can trap small birds so there are some alternatives such as straw, green waste from the kitchen or a clear plastic sheet. All these options will keep the birds at bay while at the same time aiding the germination of your grass seed. Once grass seed is down, you must try to avoid walking on it for at least six weeks, and preferably for the first few months. All seeds need water to germinate but grass seed can be tricky as too much water will kill off the seedlings. The key to this is to make sure the seeds are always moist but never wet. This is another reason why a mulch of something such as straw is such a good idea.

Follow all these steps and by the spring (or autumn if you sowed in spring) you should have a lovely new lawn.

HOW TO LAY TURF

You can lay turf at almost any time of year, although autumn and spring are generally best as the ground mustn't be too dry, frozen or waterlogged (which is why summer and winter aren't ideal). If you lay a lawn in summer, you'll need to water frequently and heavily, which will result in a hefty water bill and of course isn't good for the environment either.

Turf is sold by the square metre and is usually delivered in strips measuring about 100 x 30cm (40 x 12in). It will be rolled into bundles when it arrives. Lay these as soon as you can, otherwise the turf may turn yellow or mouldy. It should not be left rolled up for longer than two days.

Before laying the turf, prepare the site thoroughly in exactly the same way as when you're sowing grass seed, then lay the turf strips along the area to be covered, making sure there are no gaps between them and staggering the joins.

It's best to keep off the new turf for a few weeks if possible, so the grass can become established.

MAINTAINING A LAWN

The amount of time you spend maintaining your lawn once it's established is up to you – it really depends on how pristine and weed-free you want it to be. With regular feeding, weeding and mowing, and scarifying, aerating and top-dressing when required, you will have a lawn of pure grass and no weeds and moss. You can pick and choose which of the following you would like to do, depending on the finish you would like to achieve.

FEEDING

Avoid feeding the lawn after mid-summer as this will cause excessive growth into the autumn, resulting in possible damage if there is a frost. Other than that, feeding the lawn is fairly straightforward. Start in the spring, after the frost risk is over, to get the vigour straight into the lawn so that any mosses and weeds are out-competed. Always use a nitrogen-rich fertiliser, either chicken manure pellets, comfrey tea or an ammonia-based chemical feed. With the organic options, make sure you do not over feed; once every six to eight weeks is more than enough. With chemical feeds the simple advice is to always follow the packet instructions to the letter. These chemicals are strong and can be dangerous to you and your family or damaging to the plants. Following the guidelines ensures you only ever handle them in a safe way.

WEEDING

Weeds are the bane of any gardener's life; if you love a neat lawn you will tear your hair out over lawn weeds. The simple solution is to let them be. However, that will not satisfy many gardeners. The more convoluted but very effective method involves two principles. Number one, keep a healthy lawn full of vigour, that way the weeds will have less of a chance to take hold. Number two, remove any weeds once they do occur. Removing lawn weeds by hand is the most effective and environmentally friendly method but it is laborious, even with a lawn weeder, which makes the job a little easier. Alternatively, a selective herbicide will do the job. It is not as good for the environment but it will make your lawn care less backbreaking. A broadleaf weed killer will destroy most lawn weeds while having no ill effects on the grass itself. Again, always follow the instructions on the packaging but a general rule is that herbicide should be applied when the weeds are a few inches high, after the seed leaves have been replaced by slightly older leaves. If the weed is too young the herbicide will not work. If the weed is too mature, though, it will also not work, so make sure you catch it at the right time. Another way of increasing your chances of success is to make sure you do not apply weed killer in, immediately before or immediately after rain. It will wash away and you will have wasted your time and your money. Do not apply it in the extreme heat of the midday sun either, as it will evaporate. Never apply too much. It will work so quickly that it will kill the leaves before it gets to the root. Do not apply in high winds as it will blow all over the place, possibly killing off your neighbour's plants or the ones you have in the borders next to your garden. Some weed killers are painted on, in which case it does not matter much if there is any wind. The best time to apply herbicide is early in the morning or late in the afternoon on a dry but mild day with a gentle breeze.

MOWING

Your mowing regime will depend on your lawn. For a bowling-green style, perfect green, mow at least once a week all through the summer and late spring. If you are more of a 'normal but neat' kind of person then once a week or a little over should suffice. If you don't mind it getting a bit shaggy, mow it when it starts to bother you. And if you like a spring-flower meadow as opposed to a lawn then cut it in midsummer and regularly for the rest of the season. For a summer-flowering meadow, don't mow until late summer.

Different types of mower will create different effects. A cylinder mower is a neat finish where a rotary, with its propeller-type blades is slightly less so. For a really neat finish buy a mower that has a roller on the back. This will allow you to make stripes. The best mowers have adjustable blades so that in the height of the summer you can cut the grass really short and at other times more gentle cuts can be carried out. An electric mower tends to have rotary blades and the obvious thing to point out with these is that you should not cut through the wire. For those with a huge area of a lawn, a ride-on mower is a quick (and fun) but quite expensive piece of machinery that will make lighter work of mowing.

A mower will either pick up your clippings or not. The grass clippings left on the ground build up in the 'thatch' of the lawn. This can cause problems if it builds up too much but a little of it will feed the lawn. You can either rake up the clippings as required or buy a mower that picks them up for you and then scatter some clippings as an alternative to feeding. For a wildflower meadow always remove your clippings as leaving them will feed the lawn and reduce the number of flowers.

SCARIFYING

This method involves deep raking the lawn to remove the build-up of dead and decaying grass and moss from the surface. It allows more air to get to the grass's roots and encourages stronger grass growth. Ideally, scarify annually in early autumn.

AERATING

This is the best way of getting air into the grass's roots by using a fork or aerator to make holes. It is particularly important on heavy soils, which may become easily compacted. Again, it should ideally be done once a year, in early autumn (after scarifying).

TOP-DRESSING

Scattering a thin layer of lawn sand and compost and, sometimes, additional grass seed, over the lawn will make the soil richer, the existing lawn plusher, and fill any gaps without grass. It is best done in autumn, after scarifying and aerating.

The perfect lawn takes a lot of work, but I have a huge respect for a mossy, daisy-filled lawn. It's softer underfoot and quite beautiful. So don't feel guilty if you don't have the time to dedicate to this rigorous regime of lawn care. Just do what you have time for.

CHANGING LEVELS

If your garden is on a slope, you'll need at least some areas of level ground. Plants, in time, will give soil stability if it's on a gradient, so in planted areas there is no problem with having some gentle slopes. But for any hard landscape features you will need a level surface so you will need to address the gradient.

There is no denying that a change in level brings a challenge but also makes for a much more interesting design. Straight, geometric edges softened by plentiful foliage mean that you never quite know what's round the corner.

You have several options for dealing with a slope, including constructing terraces and banks. Terraces are like large steps and create level areas that can be used for a patio, lawn or planting. Each terrace is contained by a retaining wall. Constructing terraces involves quite a bit of upheaval and expense, but it's worth every penny. As well as offering a practical solution, the different levels and heights will make the garden more interesting from a design point of view.

Alternatively, you may decide to level certain areas for your hard landscaping and use the spoil from your excavations to create a bank, which can be grassed over or planted. Make sure the bank isn't too steep, or it will be difficult to mow or maintain.

You will often need to create steps to link the different levels. In the case of an extreme slope in a garden, a combination of steps and terracing might be the only solution. Steps can be an attractive feature, so consider the style you would like and your choice of materials, and make them an integral part of your design.

Where there is a gentle slope, you may like to consider installing a ramp, particularly if you need to provide access for wheelchair or buggy users, or to make moving a mower or wheelbarrow around the garden easier.

Another really attractive way of dealing with a slope is by introducing some raised beds in the form of terracing. This makes a space that would otherwise be problematic into something verdant and lush.

DECORATIVE FEATURES

Just as you would put cushions and lampshades in your house, the decorative features of a garden transform it from a practical space into something beautiful and personal. They can enhance the design, too, if you use them as focal points or to pull together a theme. And although these sorts of features are inherently aesthetic, they can also be practical. An obelisk can be used to grow a climber – even an edible climber – or a stunning pot can be used to grow herbs. So these features are worth considering from the start. Although some might be finishing touches, they are integral to the design.

A change in material or height can add a contrast that takes the viewer by surprise and adds immense visual interest.

Echoing form but using contrasting material creates harmony and cohesion.

In a large space an arbour such as this imposing one holds a space together and helps draw the eye. It does require some hefty engineering to keep it secure though.

Pergolas and arches

A pergola is a kind of tunnel that goes over a path or paving. It is usually made of timber but sometimes metal or a combination of materials is used. An arch is similar but much smaller and, as its name suggests, its top is arched rather than square. Using these features will bring height to the centre of the garden or at least away from the boundaries. Creating verticals like this draws the eye through the space very effectively. It also adds extra surfaces on which you can grow your climbers. There is nothing more beautiful in my opinion than an archway covered in plants. Those plants can then hang down above your head as you walk through. Big flowers like wisteria or laburnum work really well used in this way as do scented flowers such as honeysuckle or jasmine.

You can even grow edibles such as grapes along these sorts of structures. I once saw an archway made of living willows with their branches woven together, covered in a grapevine. As you walked along it you could pick and eat the grapes. I fell in love with this idea. Practically too, a large feature like this can add shade and shelter in the garden as well as obscuring the view to possible eyesores, while at the same time framing views you might want to enhance. It can either accentuate a view or create a small amount of shelter.

Again, there are all sorts of pre-fabricated pergolas and arches available, in varying sizes, but if you're creative and practical, you might want to build something yourself.

To fit them securely, concrete them in at the base with a quick-setting mix.

Archways and pergolas can bring height and seclusion with the introduction of some delicate climbing plants.

Alternatively hard landscape structures can create a modern finish if left exposed and geometric.

WATER

Water is a wonderful thing to include in your garden. A garden is a natural space that is full of life and water is the key component of life. It benefits you by creating a calm atmosphere and reflecting any light that bounces off it, so rather like a mirror it can lighten up a space. As well as that it also benefits all the creatures that will be using your garden, even without you knowing. From birdbaths to huge ponds, any bit of water will be of great benefit to nature. For plant lovers, having an area that includes water also allows the opportunity to grow a different range of plants from those in the rest of the garden. There are so many reasons to include water, even in tiny quantities, that there really is no excuse not to.

Ponds

A pond is one of the most basic, and one of the most effective forms of water feature. In terms of design, a large area of water will have a huge impact on the look of the garden. Whether it's using the reflections, filling it with lush aquatics or creating a wide open space with nothing but clear water, the effect will have a vast influence on the look and feel of your garden. The shape of the pond can create drama or emulate nature, depending on your choice, and a series of ponds, potentially connected by rills, which are long channels of water, can even act as barriers and become an integral part of your design. As well as all of this, a pond is a fantastic thing to include if you want to help wildlife. Insects, birds, amphibians, mammals, fish and all other kinds of species need water in order to survive.

There are a number of different ways of making a pond. I will talk you through the basic options, so you can decide what would work best in the garden you want to create.

RAISED PONDS

Raised ponds are more contemporary than the traditional-style sunken pond. They tend to be made from wood, brick or stone, although there is nothing stopping you from using other materials if you so desire. For example, metal could create an interesting effect, or you could used recycled materials such as an old butler sink or old tyres stacked on top of one another. Depending on the material you use, you may have to line the pond with a butyl liner or a thick layer of waterproofing paint, as long as there are no gaps. If the material is already watertight, there is no need for this.

Raised ponds are less friendly for wildlife than sunken ponds, simply because they are harder for animals to access and escape from than ponds at ground level, so if you're looking to attract our furry, feathered and buzzing friends, you might be better off sticking to a traditional sunken pond.

SUNKEN PONDS

If you're going to create a sunken pond, where the water is at the same level as the ground around it, you will need to line your pond with either a rigid, pre-moulded unit (made of fibreglass or plastic) or a flexible butyl sheet, which sits at the base of the hole, held down by the weight of the water above.

There are pros and cons for each type. The rigid, pre-moulded liner gives extra strength to your pond and leakages and holes are less likely than with a sheet liner. However, the butyl sheet gives you complete freedom and flexibility in terms of your design, while a rigid liner is limited to certain shapes, sizes and depths.

There is nothing stopping you, if you are torn between the aesthetic and the practical, to have a pond that has split levels – half higher than ground level, the other at ground level. Or even three levels if you wanted, perhaps if there was a slope in the garden or as part of a staircase. Ponds make for a striking design, so why not design a striking pond?

POND TIPS AND HINTS

- If you're putting in a fountain or pump and are unsure about electrics, bring in a professional. Water and electricity are a dangerous combination for a novice.

- Symmetrical, regular shapes, such as circles, squares and rectangles, will generally give a pond a more formal appearance, whether you're creating a traditional- or contemporary-style garden.

- For an informal or natural look, use irregular shapes and plant around the edges with marginal plants to blend the pond with its surroundings.

- To encourage wildlife, make sure you have a gentle slope at one end so amphibians and birds can get in and out, and add rocks and grassy banks around the edge. Ideally, the deepest part of the pond should be at least 90cm (3ft), as water at this depth will not heat up or cool down too quickly. Wildlife prefers still water to moving water.

- A modern-looking pond does not have to be unfriendly to wildlife. Rocks, a shallow edge and some plant life are all they need. They don't mind if it's a square or any other shape.

- Use a good selection of oxygenating, deep-water and floating pond plants to create a healthy ecosystem and aerate the water. It will save you spending money on filtration systems (see page 160).

- Select native plants wherever possible, and avoid growing invasive pond plants.

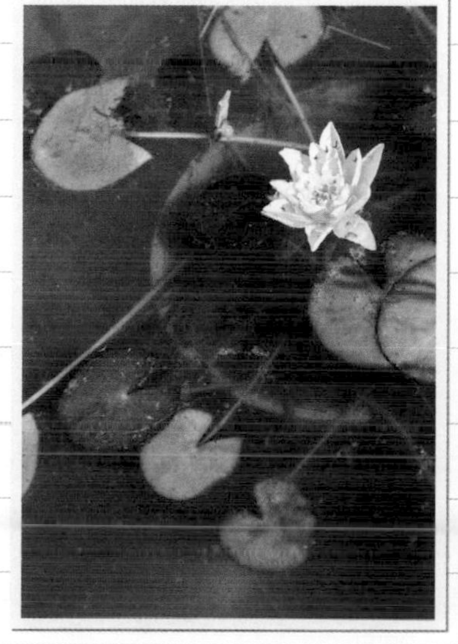

Fountains

If you buy a standalone water feature, you will probably need to have it fitted by a professional electrician. However, you can buy small fountains that are operated by a small pump and are easily installed in an existing pond.

These sorts of products come in all kinds of styles to create a range of different effects. Do not forget that there is more than one sense affected by a fountain. Obviously you can see it, but just as importantly you can hear it. Gushing waterfalls are all well and good for grand parks and monuments but I would suggest that in your back garden, a place of relaxation and escape, something gentler might be the order of the day. Most of us prefer meditation rather than invigoration.

Having said that, the look of a water feature is undoubtedly crucial. There are features that are so subtle they just create a rippling surface, others that have a more bubbling effect, and of course those that spray up into the air at varying heights. There are also fountains that fall rather than shoot up. They cascade down statues or plummet from a stone shell. Now you can even get fountains that go neither up nor down but instead shoot from one side to the other in the shape of a rainbow. The choice is vast.

HOW TO... CREATE A SUNKEN POND

- Dig a hole of the appropriate shape and size. For large fish, such as koi carp, you will need a depth of at least 1m (3ft), whereas smaller fish only need 0.6m (2ft). Aquatic plants need a range of depths so the species you want to grow will dictate your depths. Generally for marginals the minimum depth required is 0.3m (1ft) of water and a slope out of the water is preferable, if not a shelf, for the plants to sit on. Bog plants need only to sit in permanently damp soil so water a few inches deep will be more than sufficient, and for deep-water aquatics there is a whole range of required depths. In short, the more variation of depths you can include, the wider the range of plants and animals you can have in your pond.
- Check the site is flat using a spirit level. Add or remove excavated soil until the base is level.
- Clear stones or other sharp objects that may pierce the liner.
- Add a layer of sand 2.5–5cm (1–2in) thick at the base of the hole. This protects the butyl liner from hidden sharp objects and gives support to a rigid liner.
- If using a rigid liner, lower it into the hole on top of the sand bed, then pour sifted soil or fine, dry sand down the sides to support the mould.
- If using butyl liner, place a sheet of protective underlay over the sand, taking it up the sides and over the rim of the pond, then place the butyl liner over the underlay. Make neat folds, but do not worry about creases.
- Fill the pond with water using a hose. For an instant garden you may feel sorely tempted to add plants straight away. Although this will not harm the plants or the pond much, it will cause disturbance and mean that the pond takes more time to settle. Adding plants too quickly, while the water is still murky, will also mean that light does not get to the deepest depths, making some of the deep-water aquatics struggle to photosynthesise. So it is best to wait if you possibly can.

STORAGE AND UTILITY AREAS

When designing a garden, don't forget the dull but necessary elements. If you build them into your plans and make them convenient to use, they will enable you to enjoy the rest of the garden. You'll probably need to accommodate a shed, compost, areas for bins and recycling, and a washing line.

Sheds

The much-loved garden shed is incredibly useful for storing gardening equipment and also, possibly, overspill from the house.

Pre-fabricated sheds come in all shapes, sizes and materials. You can battle through the construction yourself or, where possible, ask a specialist from the company you bought it from to put it up for you. It depends how much money, time, patience and perseverance you have. And how much you mind if certain bits are put on back to front or upside-down!

If you're putting the shed up yourself, remember to create a strong foundation. Either dig a hole the same dimensions as the shed, or build up with wooden planks and fill the space with concrete. The concrete base, whether below or above ground, should be at least a few inches thick to fully support the shed and its contents. If you're digging down, it's a good idea to line your hole with wooden planks to prevent any cement soaking away into the ground and damaging the plants.

If you have grandiose schemes for building your own shed, it's worth getting the go-ahead from your neighbours. If in doubt, check local planning laws. Wooden structures tend not to need planning permission but if you are building something more permanent out of brick then it might. If the building runs along a boundary or if the walls are more than 2.5m (8ft) tall, permission might also be needed. These restrictions vary depending on your region so always research before building.

Compost

It's well worth dedicating an area to compost. In the smallest gardens, a compost heap or bin may be impractical, but generally there will be a tucked-away space to collect compostables. Even if you don't have any plants, it is likely that neighbouring trees will drop their leaves and most food waste can be composted.

There are all kinds of different composting systems and styles. Anything of a vegetative nature can go into your compost, including paper and cardboard. Grass clippings are very rich in ammonia and become slimy once they have decomposed so although adding some will make a good feed, too many will cause problems. Similarly, thick wood should be avoided. If you have the patience to chop up large pieces of wood to no wider than 2cm (0.5in) then you can include it, otherwise take it to the tip or invest in a wood chipper. Do not put perennial weed roots into the compost and if you can, try to prevent any weed seeds going in. This reduces the risk of spreading seed all over your garden when you add your compost to your soil. Finally, an excess of fruit in the compost runs the risk of attracting a lot of insects, especially wasps.

In terms of compost care, add water, make sure a bit of your soil goes in to promote a healthy population of microbes and invertebrates (if in doubt dig up a few earth worms and put them in your compost heap), keep it warm with a bit of carpet on the top and chop it up and turn it regularly.

The clearance operation

Once you've created your design and decided on the hard landscaping, it's time to clear your garden so it can undergo its great renaissance.

Do not risk your safety. If you're undertaking the clearance work yourself, always wear gloves to protect your hands from injury and vibration damage if using power tools, goggles to protect your eyes from debris and infection, a visor or face shield to protect your face from debris, and a helmet if dealing with heavy objects like bricks or branches. Steel toe-cap shoes or boots (with ankle support preferably) are also useful. Felling or pollarding trees should always be left to a professional.

Saving plants

If you have attractive herbaceous perennials or shrubs that are in the wrong position but are too good to throw away, dig up the plants carefully in winter, trying to keep as many of their roots as possible intact, and pot them up. You can keep them in their pots until you're ready to replant them, or give the potted plants away to friends and family, or even sell them (you could put them outside your house and provide an honesty box!).

Other buildings

Not many of us have the luxury to include things such as glasshouses or summerhouses in our gardens but I would urge those who have the space and the budget to invest in one. A glasshouse is not only stunning but essential for any keen grower to really maximise their productivity. A cold frame works wonders but a glasshouse protects from frost, actively heats if there is a heating method and crucially protects tender plants from the brightest sunshine. There is also nowhere nicer to be in the winter months than in a glasshouse. The ambient heat and scents are intoxicating, yet comforting. And if you are not an avid grower then a summerhouse is another great way of enabling yourself to enjoy the garden all year. With a sofa and a blanket or even a heater or wood burner, a building like this will allow you to enjoy the winter months, make the most of the limited light and still be warm and cosy. If in doubt then visit a showroom or a public garden that has such a building and see for yourself.

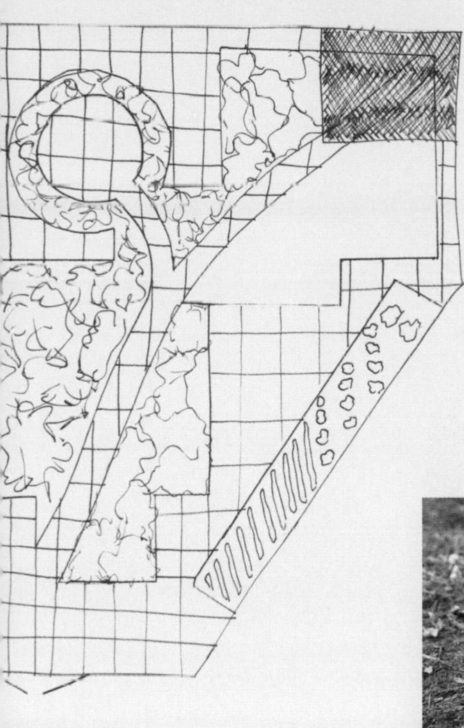

Marking out the hard landscaping areas

When creating the various hard landscaping features in the garden, it's important to take your time, refer to your plan frequently, and make sure you get it right – this will save you a lot of trouble in the future.

Once you have your ideas sorted, your plans drawn up and you are ready to go, measure out your garden in grids either with a string or canes and then make a copy of your plan to the correct size on the floor of your plot. Mark out your beds, buildings, pathways, lawns and patios. You can buy special cans of spray paint or fill bottles with sand and pour it out and in that way you can draw the plans directly onto the ground. You can scrub the lines out if you go wrong and start again and then you will get a really good sense of how the design will look once it's completed. Once you are underway with the construction this is also a really useful way of making sure you don't go wrong. When you are satisfied with the layout, hammer pegs or stakes into the ground to make the perimeters of the different features of the garden.

Before you start construction, walk through the space and try to visualise it from all angles to make sure it's right. It is also worth painting pegs a bright colour to avoid tripping over them!

HAZARDOUS WASTE

You might find some items in the garden that you will need a licensed waste disposal company to remove, as a legal requirement. Such substances and materials include asbestos, hypodermic needles, pesticides, fuels, oils and other potentially hazardous materials. If in doubt, bring in an expert. The Environment Agency can tell you what counts as hazardous waste and who can dispose of it for you. Some plants come under this category too, including giant hogweed (*Heracleum mantegazzianum*) or Japanese knotweed (*Fallopia japonica*). These are two examples of plants that are illegal to grow in the UK, and around the world there will be many more. In theory, you shouldn't buy a house with them in the garden, as they should have been destroyed before the property was sold, but sometimes they slip under the radar. Again, consult the Environment Agency to ensure you remove and dispose of them safely.

CHAPTER 4

PLANNING BEDS & BORDERS

AEONIUM 'SCHWARZKOPF'

ORNAMENTAL GRASS FOR WINTER

While the hard landscaping provides the garden's basic framework, it is the plants that soften the harsh edges and bring your garden to life. You may plant to meet a specific requirement – a strategically positioned tree can provide shade, shelter and privacy and reduce noise pollution; a dense shrub can conceal an eyesore and act as a windbreak; fragrant flowers and berries can attract bees, butterflies and birds; and edible plants provide food. However, the overriding reason why people grow plants is because of the sensory pleasure they give, enhancing any outdoor space with their shapes, colours, textures, smells and sounds. Designing a garden from scratch can be daunting and time consuming. If you feel that you are not up to the task and have the money to hire a professional designer, it can be worth the investment, even just for a consultation to help with the basics. However, I believe that with some patience, thought and hard work – and a bit of confidence – we are all capable of designing the garden we want. It may take some years to perfect, but gardening is about nothing if not patience.

PLANTING FOR VARIETY

A successful garden design includes a variety of plants of different sizes, shapes and textures that all interact together. All the selected plants need to complement and contrast with others in the scheme, and no one plant should be too dominant. You are aiming for a pleasing, balanced whole.

COW PARSLEY (ANTHRISCUS SYLVESTRIS)

SEMPERVIVUM DISPLAYS

THE FOURTH DIMENSION

When planning a border, think about what a plant will look like at different times of the year and in years to come, and what other plants around it will be doing when it is at its best. Gardeners sometimes refer to time as the 'fourth dimension'. It is essential to think about the effects of time, but impossible to predict them accurately.

Height & spread

When planning the garden, it's important to take into account the eventual height and spread of plants – remember, plants grow widthways as well as upwards, often forming increasingly large clumps. Make sure the plants you select will have sufficient space to grow so they don't overrun their neighbours, and allow enough space not just when they're planted but for a few years afterwards. This is particularly important with larger plants, such as trees and shrubs, and vigorous spreading plants, including certain bamboos that produce incredibly strong suckers from long roots that grow quite some distance from the main heart of the plant. I've been guilty of planting a bed that looks beautiful when it's first finished but within the first year or two certain things grew too much and others didn't grow as much as I had hoped and the effect was very quickly spoiled. So always do your research when choosing a plant in order to assess how tall and wide it will become as the years go on.

Variety of scale is also important for an interesting design. Think about planting in layers, and make sure you include a balanced selection of plants of differing heights to occupy each layer: trees and tall shrubs for the highest echelons; shrubs and taller perennials for the middle zone; and small perennials, annuals, biennials and bulbs for ground level. Generally, place taller plants near the back of a border except where the border can be viewed from both sides, in which case put the tallest plants in the middle so they don't block the view of other plants.

Don't be scared of using big plants. They can serve as valuable accents throughout the space. Just remember to balance them using other accents elsewhere.

FERNS COVER SHADY GROUND

LOLLIPOP TREES GIVE HEIGHT

PYRACANTHA

TUMBLING HEBE WITH ACER

Growth habit

A plant's growth habit determines its overall shape. For instance, trees may be upright and conical or columnar (as is the case with most conifers), open and rounded (such as oak), or weeping (for instance weeping cherry). Shrubs, which are generally multi-stemmed, can be upright, arching, dome-shaped, mound-forming or low-spreading. Some plants climb, while others carpet the ground.

Try to aim for a variety of habits in your garden plan, and include those that grow both horizontally and vertically to create a garden full of interest. If a plant has a particularly striking growth habit, you may want to make a feature of it, in which case don't plant anything too tall around it or in front of it so that it can be seen in all its glory.

PYRACANTHA WITH A ROSE

MOOD

Plants can create a mood in a garden in a number of ways, with movement, sound and light playing a large part. A plant that lets the wind blow through it gently, making a soft rustling sound, can have a calming, peaceful effect. Indeed, some of the most innovative planting schemes and ideas that have come about in the last decade have reflected this, with delicate-looking grasses that catch the evening sun and dance in the slightest wind. Colour is also highly instrumental in setting the mood (see page 98). Think about the mood you want to create – it can be restful or stimulating, depending on the plants you select.

Shape & texture

The diversity of shapes and textures of plant materials is immense, and has a major impact on the garden. Think of the soft, intricate fern foliage of the ever-popular *Dicksonia antarctica* compared with the sword-like leaves of New Zealand flax (*Phormium*). Although the two plants are similar in size and habit, they look entirely different because of their leaf shape and textures. Generally, the smaller and more intricate the leaves, the more delicate the plant will look, while a plant that has huge round leaves will tend to look more robust but can create a restful feel or make more of a statement, depending on how they are used. Small leaves can be a bit busy if used to excess but they will soften harsh shapes if required. Think also about how a leaf feels – is it hairy, smooth, shiny, matt, rough or waxy, and is it covered with pimples or does it have a dusting of fine powder on its surface? Different leaf textures reflect the light in different ways, a factor that also contributes to the effect of the overall planting scheme.

And it isn't just leaves that provide texture. If your garden is to look good over winter, you need to draw upon the whole spectrum of plant material – interestingly textured bark, stems that curl and corkscrew, shapely seed heads, smooth shiny berries and the thorns of a rose.

It's best to select a range of plants with contrasting textures, as this will create the most interesting designs and effects. A spear of a strong leaf blade stands out much more if it emerges from a soft haze of foliage than if it sticks up among others of its kind. The more you think about how the different textures of the plants you choose will work with each other, the more successful your borders will be.

Pinnate
Bipinnate
Tripinnate
Trifoliate
Peltate
Palmate

PLANTING FOR YEAR-ROUND INTEREST

KNIPHOFIA 'GREEN JADE'

A general rule is that one-third of the plants in a border should be **evergreen** and not lose their leaves if you want the border to look acceptable all year round. These plants can be trees, shrubs or perennials and you should choose them carefully as they will create permanent structure and accents. Always try to create some evergreen height throughout the length of the space to draw the eye. Usually your hedging will fall under this category though of course sometimes it might be deciduous.

Once you have decided on your evergreen plants then you need to move on to selecting **deciduous trees and shrubs**. Again, thinking about height early on will enable you to create a balanced design. The purpose of deciduous shrubs is to add seasonal interest. The smaller the space, the more seasons of interest a plant should have. So think about flowers, fruits, scents, autumn colour and general form. The most impactful and impressive plants will be feature plants and others might just function as a backdrop of green or another colour from which the feature plants will stand out.

The next thing to think about is **perennials**. Some of these will be feature plants if they are real show-stoppers and others will act as breaks between certain species and can blend more into the background.

The **annuals and bulbs** are the last things you will plant and are, to some extent, changeable as you can vary the displays each year.

EUONYMUS EUROPAEUS 'RED CASCADE'

PLACING PLANTS

Placing plants is a real skill. It takes years of practice so be prepared to move things around each autumn if needs be. There are, however, a few rules that can make success first time more achievable.

1. The first thing to remember is to **get your statement plants in first**. This means your evergreen structure, your specimen trees and shrubs and your hedges. This way you get a balance of height throughout the garden and you have a clearer idea where the colour accents and floral interest needs to be. Stand back in order to assess this and view it from where you will be seated most frequently.

2. The second, and possibly most important, rule is: **keep it simple**. In many ways, the fewer species of plant you use the better. Limit your colours and limit your choices. It is better to use the same plants repeatedly than introduce hundreds of different ones. If you feel something is missing you can always add it at a later date.

3. Rule three is: **plant in groups**. If you put one plant here, then another plant 3m away, with numerous other species in the intervening space, your finished garden will look bitty, busy and unrestful. It is always better to plant in groups. Some people take this to the extreme by planting in almost dead straight lines. Prairie planting often uses this ethos for ease of maintenance to very good effect, as when viewed side-on you would never know. But generally plants should be positioned either in clusters, which are circular-ish areas with the tallest plants at the back, or swathes, which are informal, often diagonal lines that slalom a little and are not uniform. Plants make much more of an impact in groups and the design will flow much more effectively.

4. The next rule is: **repetition**. Use multiple groupings of the same species or at least the same colour to draw the eye through the garden. This even applies to shrub and tree choices.

5. The final rule is to **plant using odd numbers**. In formal gardening this is not the case and symmetry works best, but for all other designs choose odd numbers. This is something to consider from the beginning when choosing your trees and specimens. Three tall accents will be much more visually effective than four. Intentional asymmetry is what our eye finds most relaxing. When placing perennials, use groups of three at a minimum and preferably groups of five or seven. Once you get about ten it doesn't make a difference if they are odd or even numbers.

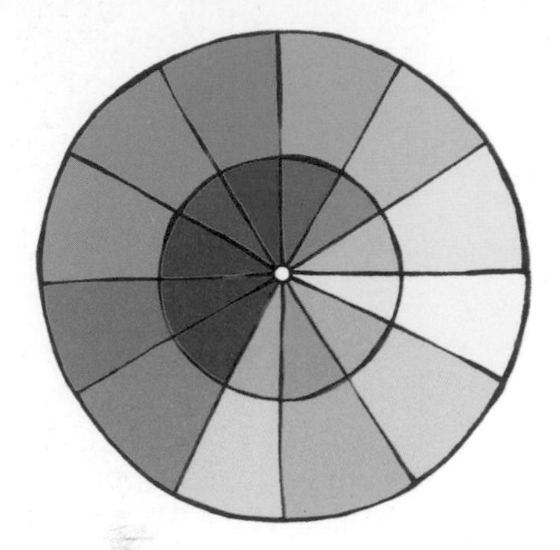

Basic colour theory

It's helpful when choosing colours for the garden to look at a colour wheel, as it shows the ways different colours relate to each other.

Colours opposite each other on the wheel are complementary, which means they produce striking contrasts that work well together. Colours that are adjacent to each other are known as analogous colours, and they will harmonise with each other and create a gentle feel. Both combinations will produce a pleasing effect.

USING COLOUR

One of the most exciting aspects of designing a new garden is deciding on the colours, as these will determine the mood to a large extent. Do you want it to be a calming, exciting, dramatic, cheerful or romantic place? You might like to refer to your mood board (see page 44) to see the kinds of colours and combinations you're attracted to. Use whatever colour scheme appeals to you, but do think about it beforehand to avoid any nasty surprises!

CERCIS CANADENSIS

COLOURFUL COLEUS VARIETIES

SAMBUCUS NIGRA 'BLACKLACE'

ALLIUM SEED HEAD

NOT JUST THE FLOWERS

When choosing the colour you're going to focus on, remember that colours do not only concern flowers. Leaves, bracts, seed heads, fruits and berries are all colourful, and you can create colour in your garden without a single flower should you wish to.

Choosing a colour theme

The best place to start is to think of a single colour that you particularly like, either because it's your favourite or because you feel it creates a certain mood or effect. Have a flick through a garden magazine and look at what colours appeal to you in a garden setting. You may surprise yourself. For instance, I would be very reluctant to wear purple clothes or paint the walls of my house purple, but I love purple plants. So have a look and decide what it is that you like in a garden. Be wary of any preconceptions that you may have – contrary to popular belief, all colours can work within the parameters of any stylistic idea. For instance, bold, bright colours can create a cottage-garden style of planting scheme, and subtle pastels can make a modern statement.

Once you've chosen your main colour, there are a number of ways that you can go on to use this colour to its best effect. I will explain a few possible methods of pairing and combining colours, and then you'll hopefully be able to decide which kinds of colour groupings will create your desired atmosphere.

1. SINGLE COLOUR THEME

The most simple and in many ways most modern use of colour is to use only your chosen colour throughout. You can use paler versions of it if you like, but in essence the only featured colour in the garden other than green will be your colour of choice. Green is an essential component of this style of design, which is good because, realistically, it's an unavoidable component of any garden! And if you want a green-only garden, that's fine. In fact, some of the most interesting gardens are created using foliage-only plants or plants that produce green flowers. If you're going to have a single colour theme, make sure you pay extra attention to the shape, habit and texture of plants you intend to use, and include plenty of variety, otherwise the result may be rather monotonous.

The classical, simple formality seen in the picture on the left uses white for extra grace, whereas the green foliage plants on the right create, quite literally, an urban jungle.

THINK PALETTE

If you're new to gardening, keep your planting ideas simple. The fewer different plants you use in the space, the more cohesive the planting will look and the easier it will be to get visually striking results. As a general rule, the fewer colours you use in your planting scheme, the more contemporary the result will be.

2. COMPLEMENTARY SCHEME

This scheme involves choosing a complementary colour to use in conjunction with your central colour. It will be immediately opposite your chosen shade on the colour wheel. The effect of a complementary scheme can be very dramatic. Tried-and-tested combinations include purple and yellow, red with green, and blue with orange. And let's not forget the sophisticated pairing of black and white. There are a few plants out there that have foliage or flowers that are nearly black as pitch, but as such run the risk of being 'lost' against dark soil, so benefit enormously from the presence of a few pale or white plants near them.

A combination that uses complementary colours is more commonly associated with modern planting schemes, especially if combined with plants with a striking form and texture. But using a complementary combination for plants with a delicate, fluffy texture and an inconspicuous growth habit can create a border that is traditional but with a bit of an unexpected twist. Also, by using pastel tones rather than purer or brighter colours it's easy to create something surprisingly subtle and pastoral.

You'll also need to consider the colour green. In most combinations, green foliage plays a very important role, softening the design and acting as a foil for other colours. However, in a combination that has the potential to be extremely striking, green can lessen that effect, so you may prefer to choose plants with foliage in other colours. If you have a flower that is a striking yellow, then a green backdrop could minimise the intensity of its colours. Try growing a purple foliage plant like *Lysemachia* behind it. Some plants naturally combine complementary colours; the *Dahlia* 'Bishop of Canterbury' is yellow and purple and *Lobelia cardinalis* combines green with a striking red flower.

Purple and yellow is a classic combination that creates cheerful drama (right).

3. HARMONIOUS SCHEME

A harmonious scheme involves choosing an analogous colour to use with your chosen colour. Select a colour immediately next to your central shade on the colour wheel, or a lighter shade of the same tone. This is an almost failsafe method, and as such may be a good scheme to start with in your first garden (you can always add accent plants in complementary colours at a later date if you find your palette is falling flat).

Generally, the finished effect of a harmonious scheme will be one of calm and relaxation. It won't challenge the eye too much, and therefore the brain will subconsciously be able to relax. For this reason, the tendency is for a colour theme of this type to create a traditional feel in a garden. However, this is not necessarily always the case. Bold, vibrant colours used in this way, or striking foliage – or indeed both – will invariably lead to a space that feels contemporary.

I do have one word of warning: be aware of leaves in colours other than green. With colours that are similar but not exactly the same there is a risk of clashing, and while green leaves tie a harmonious scheme together and act as a buffer between colours, throwing coloured foliage into the mix can be very difficult to pull off successfully. However, if you're confident with colour by all means try it – unusual combinations can be the difference between beauty and brilliance.

Where yellow offsets purple with a bang, pink or blue tones create a softer, more romantic feel using this harmonious scheme.

4. TRIAD SCHEME

For this scheme you select three colours that are evenly spread around the wheel; if you were to draw a line between them it would form an equilateral triangle. These colours all have a relationship that is strong but subtle. The easiest way of using this method would be to use green, violet and orange. There will always be green in the garden anyway, because of foliage, so if you were to use three alternatives (say yellow, red and blue) it runs the risk of being overcomplicated by the addition of the inevitable green. Still, if you feel brave enough to try it then go for it – the results could be spectacular.

Silvery blue is offset to stunning effect by the pinks and soft yellows behind it.

5. SPLIT COMPLEMENTARY SCHEME

This works in a similar way to a complementary scheme, but rather than using the colour directly opposite in the wheel, you use the two colours next to the complementary colour. A split complementary scheme creates an effect that does bring out the different colours but not to the full extent, so the final result is a little more understated. This can have the benefit of toning down a very modern scheme or slightly modernising a traditional or cottage garden design by giving it a refined edge, alluding to a vibrant contrast without quite achieving it, leaving your brain to do a little more work.

Here yellow is the main colour and is complemented by varying shades of purple and blue.

6. WARM COLOUR SCHEME

A warm scheme simply uses shades from the warm half of the colour wheel. This runs from yellow to violet/red, with a few anomalies depending on the exact shade of a colour. By using only these colours you will create a space that is warm and welcoming. A design of this type can be tempered with cooler foliage plants if you wish, or exploited for its full heat by using leaves with warm tones.

From foliage to flower, all colours here are on the warm side.

7. COOL COLOUR SCHEME

Using only colours from the cool half of the wheel, running from blue/green to violet, this scheme creates a cohesive feel throughout the space and can range from the traditional to the cutting edge. Using exclusively cool plants can give the space a really stylish finish. Alternatively, try combining it with some burnt colours like a tawny brown/orange or a deep burnt crimson to really bring out the cool tones.

Silvers, blues and purples work together to great effect.

TYPES OF BORDER

You may read or hear about different styles of border and wonder what the terms mean. Here are just some of the most familiar ones.

MIXED BORDERS

The most popular choice for gardens, mixed borders contain a bit of everything – trees and shrubs to give height and structure, and perennials, annuals and bulbs for colour and filling gaps. There is something to see throughout the year in a well-planned mixed border.

FLOWER BORDERS

Only herbaceous perennials, annuals and biennials are used. Flower borders require more maintenance than mixed borders, and once the display is over there is little to see.

SHRUB BORDERS

A low-maintenance option, only small trees and shrubs are used in a shrub border.

ANNUAL BEDDING SCHEMES

Only annuals are used, so although you'll have a bright, colourful flower display the plants will need replacing at least once every year.

GRASS AND PERENNIAL BORDER

This is a relatively new planting style. Grasses are the main plants, combined with some hardy herbaceous perennials, and plants are usually arranged in strips. Prairie borders are fairly low maintenance, as everything can be cut back with shears once a year in late autumn.

HERBACEOUS BORDERS

This style of border uses only herbaceous perennial flowering plants and became popular in the late Victorian period. Generally there is less flower power than in a floral border but the maintenance is easy, cutting most if not everything back in the autumn, almost to the ground. In some areas of the world these borders are even mown annually.

Your choice of hard landscaping will probably lend itself to a particular style of border. To create a successful design you need to ensure both the hard and soft landscaping work together.

Don't worry!

Planning the planting can be tricky, and what may seem perfect in theory may not work out quite the way you want in reality – every garden is different, plants grow at different rates, flowers bloom at unexpected times, and plants are living things that have a mind of their own. Like children and pets, they don't always behave themselves!

When I was an apprentice, my mother kindly gave me a small patch of our garden to experiment in. To this day, when I go back home and look at the patch I created I cringe, as it's a mess. Certain things now take up the whole space and other plants that I was so proud of at the time are all but dead. However, I learnt more from my mistakes than my successes, as do all new gardeners, so good has come out of it after all.

The great benefit of plants over hard landscaping is that they are changeable and moveable. Planting schemes can be added to over time. Over years even. You can leave gaps where you have yet to decide what will go there, or you can simply dig up and rearrange areas that you aren't happy with. Just remember, gardening is all about trial and error.

Creating a planting plan detailing the exact positions of the plants will help you greatly when you are planning, planting and maintaining the garden in years to come. A plan also makes a great reference if you struggle to remember exactly how to prune, propagate from or even use the plants you have chosen as you can always go back and research. It also makes you feel much more confident if you have it all written down.

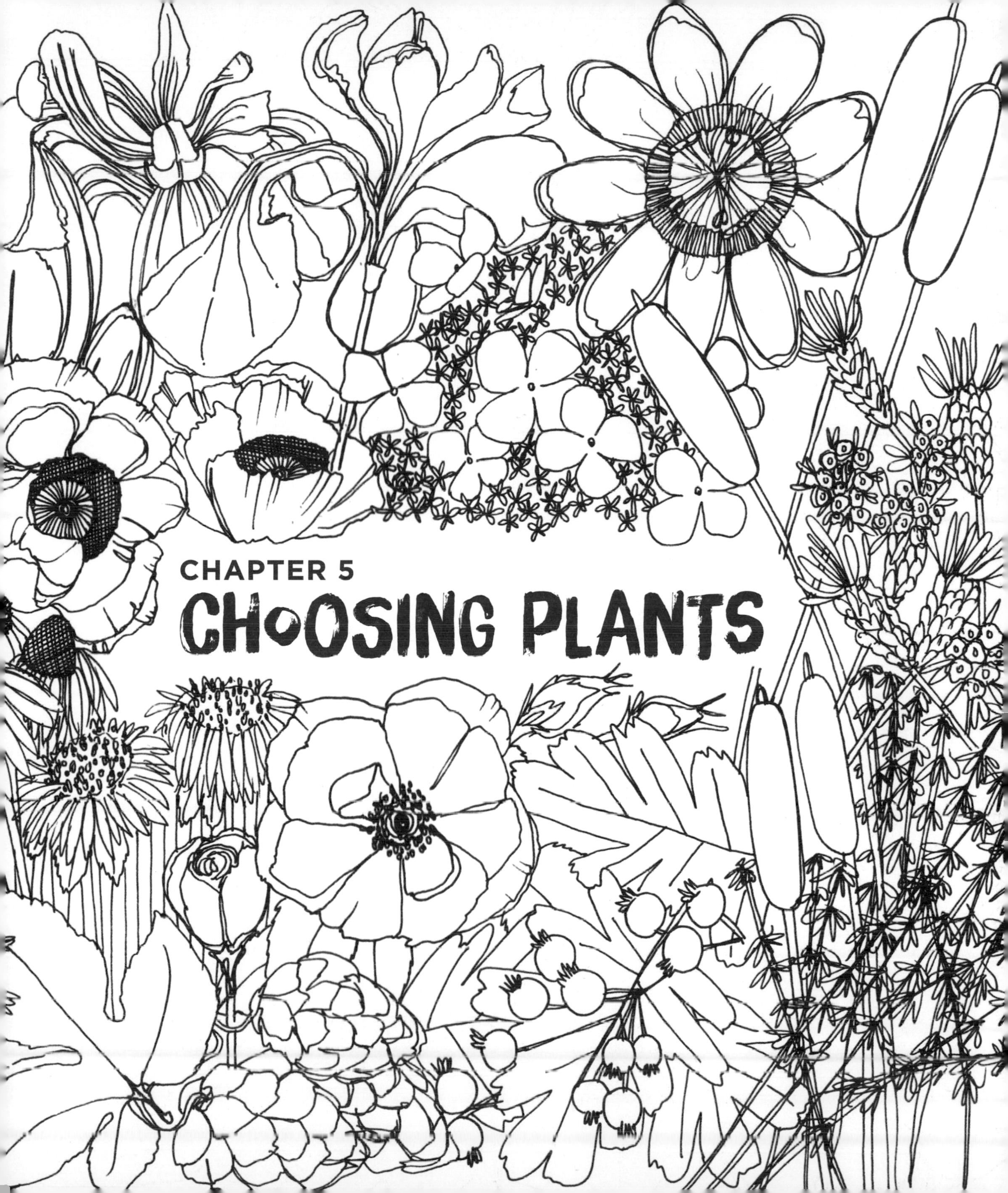

CHAPTER 5
CHOOSING PLANTS

In this chapter I have selected a range of plants that are great for first-timers. I'll explain what you need to know about them so you can assess if they're right for you and your space. That way, you'll avoid the common pitfall of going to the garden centre or nursery and picking what 'looks nice'. The key is to choose plants that thrive in the conditions your garden offers and avoid those that don't, or that require more maintenance than you're able to provide.

AT-A-GLANCE GUIDE TO PLANT TYPES

It's really helpful to know the different types of plant you can expect to find so you can understand how they grow and how to use them in planting schemes. These terms are all used on plant labels and in catalogues.

NEWLY PLANTED 'STANDARD' TREE

COTINUS COGGYGRIA 'ROYAL PURPLE'

TREES Generally the largest and most prominent features in the garden, trees are woody plants that usually grow from one central stem, or trunk.

SHRUBS These are woody plants, with a permanent structure of woody stems and branches above the ground. They resemble trees but have several or many stems growing from the base rather than a single trunk. Shrubs that never get very tall are called sub-shrubs. They look like a perennial but have a woody base.

CLIMBERS Plants that climb up a support, such as a wall, fence, trellis, post, obelisk, or host plant, in one of several ways (see page 140).

PERENNIALS Also known as herbaceous plants, perennials die down each autumn (except evergreen perennials) and grow up again the following spring. All the growth is green and fleshy, from soil level to the tip, with no woody tissues.

ANNUALS These live for one growing season and are disposed of at the end of the season. They germinate, flower and set seed all in less than one year. Many bedding plants are annuals.

BIENNIALS As their name suggests, biennials have a two-year life cycle. They will put on leafy growth in the first year and will flower the following year, then set seed and die. Generally, biennials are disposed of after flowering.

PINUS (PINE TREE)

BULBS A collective term used to describe plants that have an underground food storage organ. It includes true bulbs, corms, tubers and rhizomes.

GRASSES Annuals or perennials in the Poaceae family, with long, slender leaves (deciduous or evergreen) with parallel veining and often light, feathery flowerheads.

DECIDUOUS PLANTS These shed their leaves annually at the end of the growing season and replace them in spring.

EVERGREEN PLANTS As their name suggests, these retain their leaves throughout the year.

SEMI-EVERGREEN PLANTS Also sometimes referred to as semi-deciduous, these keep their leaves in a mild winter, or in a sheltered site, but lose them in cold conditions.

BEDDING PLANTS This term refers to a very varied bunch of plants that add instant colour to seasonal displays. They are disposed of at the end of the season. Traditionally annuals and biennials, in recent years the range of plants has increased and the term also includes tender perennials, bulbs and even small shrubs.

VIOLA (PANSY)

TREES

There is nothing quite like sitting beneath a tree on a summer's day, looking up at the leaves rustling in the breeze and listening to the sound of birdsong. All gardens, however small, should include at least one tree. They offer so much value in so many different ways.

MOUNTAIN ASH/ROWAN (SORBUS)

As trees are long-lived and the largest plants in your garden, they make a huge visual impact and create a sense of permanence. They provide structure throughout the year and that all-important third dimension – height, providing interest above eye level. Highly ornamental, trees are available in a vast range of shapes and sizes, and many produce beautiful leaves (deciduous or evergreen), flowers, fruits or bark. So you have a great deal of choice and should find a tree to suit your needs and garden style.

There are also numerous practical benefits of planting trees in the garden. They provide shade and shelter from the wind and protection from frost by reducing the wind-chill factor and can screen an unsightly view, maybe beyond your boundary, and help preserve your privacy. Many also make good hedges (see pages 132–135). Trees are also incredibly beneficial to wildlife, offering a home for birds, protection from predators and a source of food. In addition, they're good for the environment, improving the air we breathe and absorbing pollution and noise. Once they're established, they require little attention.

Trees are a fantastic and versatile addition. However, you should think carefully about how many you plant and where to plant them. Trees will grow tall and often spread quite wide. They will cast shade and they will add shelter. These may be assets but they may also be causes of irritation if you plant something that all but excludes your sunlight, for example. Think about the species of tree you wish to plant and choose one that will not outgrow its position. But also think about strategic positions to place those trees.

A specimen tree grown as a focal point in the garden should be planted, if not in isolation, certainly far enough away from other trees that it makes a statement. It should also aim to provide you with interest throughout the year, or when you will be using the garden the most.

Trees can be used along a boundary to create privacy or reduce noise and air pollution. Think about the neighbours when you plant trees in this way and choose species that will not damage foundations with strong exploratory roots (such as fig trees) or that will not cast too much shade into your neighbours' gardens. Even small trees make a huge difference to noise levels. For a modern look, you may want to stick to one or two species but for maximum benefit to wildlife, and to increase the seasons of interest, use a variety of species that peak at different times but still work together.

To create a little height in accents throughout the garden, try using odd numbers. In a small garden one tree might be enough. Either place it where you want to maximise your privacy, or where it will have the most visual impact – usually at the edge of the garden or a few feet in. If you have slightly more space then try using three trees and stagger them along the length of the garden with two on one side and one on the other. Odd numbers are always more pleasing to the eye, even in a modern planting scheme. For formality, even numbers placed symmetrically will be more effective but be aware that this will shorten your space visually. In a large garden you have the opportunity to play with accent trees. Try using opened umbrellas or stakes of wood in different patterns then view them from the house and any other important points in the garden to get an idea of the most effective arrangement. One good-sized tree will enhance your space much more than lots of trees that never quite get big enough. But do be realistic when planting. Unless you have a gargantuan budget you will not be able to afford to plant fully mature specimens and smaller trees will grow better in the long run. Be patient when watching your garden develop.

Dig a generous-sized hole, plant the tree, never too deeply but always in a hole at least a third wider than the root ball, and for the first year keep the roots moist with periodic soaking that allows water right down into the base rather than just a superficial soaking at the surface. This will allow the roots to grow down more deeply and offer greater anchorage for the tree. You may also want to stake the tree. Make sure the stake is no taller than a third of the way up the tree.

I have chosen a few trees to describe in detail. Some are my personal favourites, others are based on practical considerations. There should be something for everybody.

MOUNTAIN ASH/ROWAN (*Sorbus aucuparia*)

The mountain ash is steeped in mythology. It is said that to have one in your garden will bring good spirits and protect your land and family. Of course that is not really the reason why the species is one of my favourites. In fact, I love this tree because it offers so much in a small space. As a member of the rose family it both flowers with prolific blossoms in the spring and fruits in the autumn with a feast for the birds. The leaves turn a gorgeous shade of orange/red in the autumn and contain multiple leaflets – like an ash tree, hence its common name. It is a fantastic choice for the domestic garden because it will never get too big. As a medium-sized tree it is perfect for even a compact garden.

There are a number of different varieties that offer a choice of colours in terms of the foliage (from silver/blue through to the richest green) and berries (most commonly bright red but also in yellow as seen on 'Joseph Rock' and pearlescent pink on the *Sorbus vilmorinii*).

Look at as many different varieties as you can before deciding on one and you will enjoy this tree for years to come. The

CHERRY TREE IN AUTUMN

eventual size will vary according to variety but the dimensions of the common Rowan are as follows:
Height: 10–12m
Spread: 4–8m
Position: sun/partial shade in acidic or neutral soil
Hardiness: fully hardy

CHERRY
(Prunus spp.)

The cherry is another example of a member of the rose family that is wonderfully useful in the garden. It produces blossom in the spring, either with single or double flowers depending on the variety. The single blossoms will then go on to produce fruit and the double flowers will not. These flowers come out before the foliage, which makes for an impressive display. Depending on the variety, the new foliage can be a deep burgundy in colour and many of the cherry species (particularly the non-fruiting varieties) will have a magnificent display of autumn colour at the end of the summer, with peach/pink/orange colours that seem to glow. *P. serrula* has the most stunning red bark that brings colour to the garden even in the deep winter.

I love these trees and like to bring in the birds so I go for a species such as *P. padus* or *P. avium*. If you have a lawn, the fruit can make a bit of a mess when mowing, and they can also attract wasps causing some issues if there are children around. In these cases consider planting an ornamental cherry such as 'Pink Perfection' or 'The Bride'. Generally ornamental cherry blossom is white or pale pink, but some can also come in a vivid pink verging on cerise.

And while we are talking about the *prunus* family, look at plums and even apricots as an alternative. All of these trees will flower in spring, fruit in the autumn and none will get too big for a small garden. In short, they will work hard for you and really earn their place in even the smallest space.

MALUS (CRAB APPLE)

Height: 10–12m
Spread: 10m
Position: full sun on any soil
Hardiness: fully hardy

CRAB APPLE
(Malus spp.)

The crab apple will grace any garden and take pride of place in a small garden. These trees blossom like their close relatives, the cherries, and never get too big for their allotted space. But unlike the cherry, it is not the autumn colour that makes this tree a joy to behold towards the end of the season, but its prolific production of fruit that sits on the trees throughout the autumn and gives the garden a real zest of colourful energy when most other plants are giving up the ghost. The branches are often so laden with fruit that it is hard to see the stems themselves.

Two of the most effective colours are yellow, as seen in 'Golden Hornet' and the red that is epitomised by 'Red Sentinel'. These fruits can also be used to make jelly.

If you are interested in growing fruit for cooking, it might also be worth thinking about the common apple (of which the varieties are too numerous to list and are increasing in number) but which produce perfectly edible apples that do not need preserving. These trees are also *Malus* species, a sister species of the crab apple. If you have the space, try growing both as the crab apple encourages a wider range of pollinators, giving your eating/cooking apples a more plentiful harvest.

Height: 4–8m
Spread: 4–8m
Position: sun/partial shade in any soil type
Hardiness: fully hardy

FOREST PANSY *(Cercis canadensis)*

The forest pansy is a stunning tree. It is a small species, ideal for a city garden or a position near the house as it is decorative but does not bring in the wasps and bees as trees in the rose family tend to do. The leaves are also a real showstopper. They are cordate (heart-shaped) and generous and hang delicately from the branches.

The name was given because of the delicate, pansy-like purple/pink flowers that adorn the species in the spring. This tree will give graceful elegance and colour for most of the year and never outgrow its position. It is a must-have in any garden in terms of its ability to decorate without overpowering any garden.

Height: 8–12m
Spread: 8m+
Position: sun/partial shade in any soil
Hardiness: fully hardy

KATSURA TREE *(Cercidiphyllum japonicum)*

Do not confuse this species with forest pansy. Although there are similarities (hence the name *cercidiphyllum*, which means leaves like a *cercis*) this is an entirely separate species and behaves very differently. It is bigger for a start and needs more acidic soils that the *cercis*. It is also hardier to some extent, although both species will be fine in a temperate climate. But the Katsura tree has to be one of my all time favourites. On paper it may not quite tick as many boxes as the forest pansy – its flowers, for example, are insignificant – but there is not a species of tree that can beat it in the autumn.

I am not a big fan of autumn, but this tree is one of the things that gets me through the darkening months. The butter-yellow colour that some years verges on pink or peach is simply breathtaking, but that is not the only thing I love. It is a little known fact that it is the amount of sugar in the leaves that dictates the colour of the autumn show. In a warm and, crucially, bright summer the leaves accumulate sugar that then gives a brilliant colour to trees that show it in the autumn. The Katsura tree plays a clever trick with this sugar. Not only does it have the amazing colour but in the autumn after a warm summer it gives off the most tremendous smell of candyfloss. It is a burning sugar fragrance that is unlike anything else I have ever smelt from a tree. The delicate foliage, the graceful habit and the striking colour hugely add to its charms but the heady scent that travels for metres is the real showstopper for me. Try it and you will not be disappointed.

Height: 12m
Spread: 8m
Position: sun/partial shade in an acid or neutral soil
Hardiness: fully hardy

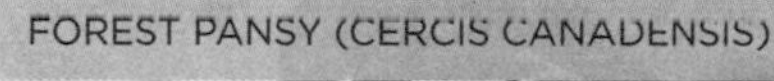
FOREST PANSY (CERCIS CANADENSIS)

MAGNOLIA

Here is a tree that will give you a magnificent show in the spring and then become a bit of a shrinking violet for the remainder of the year. For this reason I would recommend it be used in conjunction with other trees or at least shrubs that give a little more year-round interest. But who can overlook the stunning magnolia flowers?

These trees may look highly ornate and sophisticated but in fact they are some of the oldest flowering plants on the planet. They hail from a time when to be big was to be successful as it increased a plant's chances of being pollinated. This means that the flowers, which appear on bare stems, are incredibly large. They range from stunning shades of purple, through to pink and white.

The spring magnolias are not scented but if you opt instead for a *M. grandiflora* that flowers in the height of summer (although technically it may be considered more of a shrub) then you will find scent in abundance and a flower that is more of a soft shade of yellow than the pink of its spring cousins. Either one has its merits. The spring-flowering magnolia trees will have their moment and then sink into the background, losing foliage in the autumn, which has no seasonal colour, whereas the summer-flowering large shrubs hold on to their glossy, dark foliage all year round, making them a good backdrop plant that will enhance the look of others.

The trees will generally have the following dimensions and requirements.

Height: 18m
Spread: 10m
Position: sun/partial shade, sheltered
Hardiness: hardy

SILVER BIRCH
(Betula spp.)

There are a number of species of birch that are a valuable asset to any garden. The most common in Europe are the silver birch (*Betula pendula*) and the downy birch (*Betula pubescens*). Both are very similar in appearance with a white stem and small leaves that turn yellow before they fall in the autumn. The downy birch has small hairs on the leaf stalks and the silver birch has a more weeping habit but other than that the difference is minimal.

BETULA UTILIS VAR. JACQUEMONTII

The tree that has really surpassed this in modern garden design is the Himalayan birch (*Betula utillis var. jacquemontii*), which has stems that are pure white in cultivation, though in the wild the same species has deep brown stems in certain regions. We tend to grow Himalayan birch as multi-stemmed specimens because it is the stem that is so attractive. Whether it is the silver birch, downy birch or the Himalayan birch, *Betula* is one of the most graceful deciduous trees. It will create a lovely dappled shade without blocking too much light. I highly recommend this tree, especially if you have the space to plant it en masse. A small copse of birch can make a really striking feature.

Height: 12m+
Spread: 8m+
Position: sun/partial shade in any soil
Hardiness: fully hardy

OLIVE
(Olea europaea)

Olive trees are not only useful if you fancy trying your hand at the good life, but are also stunning in appearance – and evergreen, which is rare for a non-coniferous species. They are slightly tender so will either need protecting from the hardest frosts or planting in a container and kept near a south-facing wall or near the house. They are easy to

OLEA EUROPAEA GROWN AS A FAN

look after and need little to no watering, being from a Mediterranean climate. A container is often the best place for an olive tree unless you live in a very dry spot or have particularly free-draining soil.

The lovely thing about olive trees is that they can be cut back to be kept at the size you want. In fact, the most attractive olive trees are the ones that have thick, gnarly trunks but with short, fine new stems at the crown and are no taller than 3m (10ft).

Height: 10m (but can be pruned lower)
Spread: 10m
Position: full sun
Hardiness: hardy to -10°C or thereabouts

HAZEL
(Corylus avellana)

Having grown up in Kent I couldn't write a book without including the humble Kentish cobnut (or hazel as it's known everywhere else). I love these trees because they are so multi-functional. Not only do they produce a delicious nut that is tasty straight from the tree – or dried and put into a chocolate bar – but they also have the most fantastic branches that are both strong and flexible, making them ideal for building and in particular, fencing and even basket weaving. For any farmstead or smallholding this tree is a must-have. It will become a sizeable tree if left unchecked, but with coppicing every three to five years the hazel will stay small enough that it will not become a problem. In this way it can even be used as a hedge and bent to make a traditional hedgerow.

This coppiced wood also makes great fuel for a fire so this is a fantastic tree for anybody with a wood fire or who enjoys the occasional bonfire.

NB If you want your hazel to bear fruit then you will need to have two or more hazel trees as the species is not self-fertile, which means it cannot mate with itself.

Height: 4–8m (can be coppiced and kept smaller)
Spread: 4–8m
Position: sun/partial shade in alkaline or neutral soil
Hardiness: fully hardy

MAPLE
(Acer spp.)

Maples are a genus of deciduous tree often (though not always) with palmate leaves. So how do you spot a maple? Well, there are two defining features which, if seen in combination, are a sure sign that you are looking at a maple. Firstly, all maples have winged seeds. If you played with 'helicopters' as a child, which involved throwing certain seeds into the air and watching them spiral downwards like a helicopter, then you were playing with maple seeds. All maples have seeds like this of varying sizes. The second characteristic is that all maples have opposite stems, which means that where one stem breaks away from a branch, there will always be another stem breaking off in the opposite direction in exactly the same place. This is easily seen when there are no leaves on the trees and the buds are clearly visible on the stems.

There are so many forms of maple that to group them all under one tree category is almost cheating. They are also by no means small. Some, famously the sycamore (*Acer pseudoplatanus*), actually grow to be large trees. The Norway maple grows to become a large, though very attractive tree. *Acer saccharinum*, another lovely maple, grows quite large and has a silvery trunk and beautiful autumn colour. As a general rule, though, acers are a species of garden tree that can often be small, delicate and elegant and as such are justifiably popular.

One of the most popular maples is the Japanese maple (*Acer japonicum*). This species is simply stunning and small enough to fit in any sized garden. It has leaves that look like lace and come in all shades of red and purple as well as green plus stems of varying and

ACER PALMATUM 'BLOODGOOD'

beautiful shades. Similar, though with less decorative leaves, is *Acer palmatum*. This grows to comparable heights and comes in nearly identical shades, but its foliage gives it a slightly more robust form.

If bark is your thing then look at *Acer griseum* and *Acer capillipes*. The latter has bark that looks like the scales of a beautiful snake with shades of pale blue, silver and even purple, as well as green. *Acer griseum* is known as the 'paper bark maple' and has bark that peels from the trunk in delicate strips. This species also has lovely trifoliate leaves, which turn a stunning red colour in the autumn.

Maples are a popular choice for good reason. The range of species means that there is no one size, so it is well worth doing your research before purchasing a maple. Generally they are small and, apart from a few large varieties, you shouldn't be in for a nasty shock. An awful lot of maples do need acidic soil. They also often benefit from a degree of shelter from the wind and sun as they can suffer from leaf scorch if they are in an exposed and bright position. If you do not have an acidic soil then an acer will quite happily survive in a container or raised bed filled with the appropriate soil so there really is nothing stopping you.

LIME TREE
(Tilia cordata)

A lime tree is wonderfully versatile. There are very few trees that can cope with the variety of situations that this species can tolerate. This is because lime trees are very good at something called epicormic growth. That basically means that a lime tree can sprout new stems anywhere down its trunk. The upshot of this skill is that the tree can be cut back as hard as you like. In this sense it can be used as a small tree with a lollipop-style head, a tall stately tree of at least 12m in height or even a pleached hedge. Pleaching is a technique whereby the branches of the tree are pulled out and tied to a wooden framework so that after some years of strategic training and pruning the tree grows to form a perfectly flat screen-like structure that can serve as a barrier to your neighbours or to certain areas of the garden that for aesthetic reasons you want shielded from view. This may sound grand but with a lime's ability to withstand a hard prune, this style of hedge can be kept to modest proportions.

The tree has cordata (heart-shaped) leaves, which are a translucent, bright green in colour and generously rotund. There are other varieties that show slightly different characteristics. *T.* x *europaea* for example, has bright red stems on the new growth. But they do all have the ability to withstand a prune.

All lime trees attract aphids. This can be extremely beneficial if you like to keep the aphid away from your more precious edible plants, but do be warned not to ever plant a lime tree immediately above where you intend to either hang your washing or park your car. The aphids act as a funnel channelling the sugars from the leaves through their body, out the other end and onto anything below it in a sticky substance that is a nightmare to remove.

If you live in a coastal area or would prefer a tree that holds on to its leaves all year round, then a good alternative for the lime tree is a holm or holly oak (*Quercus ilex*). This tree has the same properties in terms of its pruning and can be grown as a hedge, in columns, pleached, or as a tree of great stature if required.

Height: 12m+
Spread: 8m+
Position: sun or partial shade in any sheltered position in neutral–alkaline soil
Hardiness: fully hardy

LIME TREE (TILIA CORDATA)

WILLOW
(Salix spp.)

Willows grow quickly and they grow large. That is often the first thing anyone will tell you about them. And that is the reason why they have become a little out of fashion in recent years. Do not be put off though. Willows offer a wonderfully versatile choice of tree for those who are trying to plant up a very wet garden, such as one on a floodplain or marsh land, for example. Willows thrive in moist soils, probably better than almost any other tree. Waterlogging, which is one of the biggest killers of trees, is not a problem for the willow. In recent years, extreme weather has affected an increasing number of people and sudden floods and surges have wreaked havoc in gardens. Planting trees such as willow can actually help to alleviate the problems of flooding as a willow tree can consume 50–100 gallons of water a day (depending on its size).

WEEPING WILLOW

So there is a good ecological reason for planting these trees, especially if you live somewhere prone to flooding. I am also a fan of the willow tree for many other reasons. Maybe it's because of having *The Wind in the Willows* read to me as a child, but for me there is always something romantic about seeing a weeping willow. It conjures up images of hazy summer afternoons. The way they catch the wind is unlike anything else.

Even willows that grow into big trees can be pruned hard, known as pollarding, periodically to keep them in check. Others can be cut back to a stump each year and used as hedging. Many of these species have colourful stems in black, red, orange and yellow. Then there is the pussy willow, *Salix caprea*, which has buds that look like small white balls of fur. They are beautiful as trees, especially if kept small, but also make great Christmas decorations or additions to bunches of flowers if cut.

TREES & SHRUBS IN SMALL SPACES

Although you might think a tree would take up more room than a shrub in the garden, that isn't always the case. A deciduous, lollipop-shaped tree on a tall stem provides valuable growing space beneath, whereas a large, densely spreading shrub offers no ground space underneath for other plants. Think carefully about the growth habit of trees or shrubs before making any decisions.

Willow will propagate amazingly easily. The seeds (as with most moisture-loving plants) need to be used as soon as they come off the tree. Taking cuttings, however, couldn't be easier. Simply cut off the stems in the winter, chop them up making sure each segment both starts and ends at a bud and stick the stems (the right way up) in either cutting compost or water. Another option, and one of my favourite features, is to chop off a stem, making sure that there is a bud at the bottom, and then stick it into the earth where it will grow. From there it can be woven, bent and trained to form a hedgerow, a screen or even an arch.

The speed at which willow grows also makes it a fantastic source of biofuel. It is often grown in huge paddocks and coppiced as often as every three years. These removed stems can be burnt or used for basket weaving or fencing.

Height: 12m+
Spread: 8m+
Position: sun in a moist soil of any type
Hardiness: fully hardy

DOGWOOD (*Cornus spp.*)

I have often walked around a garden and been beguiled by a tree that I do not know. And more often than not, I have found I have been admiring a *cornus*.

There are the dogwoods that are used to provide winter interest with stems of varying colours, cut back each year to keep them compact for a winter display of fiery red, bright yellow, silver or deep black. There are the species such as *C. kousa* that have beautiful white flower-like bracts that cover almost the entire tree when they come out. There is *Cornus mas*, which bears bright yellow flowers in the early spring and sets fire to any garden. *Cornus controversa*, or the wedding cake tree has tiers of branches that produce a beautiful shape that can be either modern, adding horizontal architecture to a design, or traditional, using the delicate foliage as a backdrop instead. And *Cornus drummondii* produces sprays or pearly white berries in the autumn.

The range and variations is startling, but this is a genus that deserves investigation and a home in most gardens.

COLD TOLERANCE IN PLANTS

In temperate areas, not all plants can be left outside all year round. Each plant has its own degree of tolerance, and if temperatures are too low for a particular plant it can be damaged or even die. Below are definitions of terms often used to describe plants. Bear in mind that they are guidelines only, and many other considerations affect a plant's overall hardiness.

HARDY Can tolerate frost.

HALF-HARDY Will tolerate a degree of coldness – usually to between -5 and -10°C. They will need some protection in winter, e.g. cover the plant in fleece

TENDER Will not tolerate frost.

RIGHT PLANT RIGHT PLACE

This key will give you an idea about a plant's preferred habitat. Seeing one of these characteristics in a plant will help guide you and seeing them in combination will tell you almost definitely where a plant will want to be. Always read the labels of the plants you buy, too, then you know you can't go wrong.

SHADE TOLERANT
Big leaves, fine leaves, deep green colour, small flowers, pale flowers, scented flowers.

SUN LOVERS
Small leaves, silver foliage, big flowers, brightly coloured flowers, spicy or herby scented foliage.

MOISTURE LOVERS
Aerial roots, hollow stems, pithy stems, seeds that need sowing fresh.

DROUGHT TOLERANT
Succulence, spikes, hairs on foliage, pale and waxy leaf surface, rosette or spiral growth habit.

WIND TOLERANT
Bendy branches or stems, thick cuticle on leaf, small/reduced foliage.

If you plant varieties that enjoy your garden's conditions then you will have happier, healthier plants and save yourself a lot of money and work in replacing or nursing unhappy plants.

CONIFERS

Conifers are quite contemporary in terms of design – or they can be if they are used cleverly. The spear-like form of a Mediterranean cypress piercing the sky will give height and a uniform colour scheme, especially if used en masse as a backdrop or hedge for instance. Apart from a few exceptions, like the maidenhair tree, conifers keep their leaves all year, which makes them a great choice for those who don't want to spend hours picking up leaves each autumn.

MAIDENHAIR TREE (GINGKO BILOBA)

Conifers have fallen slightly out of favour over recent years. That is largely due to the fact that a few have been misused, usually as hedging that either gets far too big for its allotted space or turns brown and dies due to over-clipping. The truth is that conifers can be stunning trees. Sadly, most will not tolerate being clipped very much, so the traditional conifer hedge may not be the best way of exploiting the full potential of these plants. Instead, try using them as specimen trees. If you have a large space to play with they will truly enhance your garden all year round as they can grow to gargantuan proportions. And if you only have a modest space you will be pleasantly surprised to hear that an awful lot of these trees will thrive in a container that will stunt their growth and prevent them from outgrowing their space.

If foliage and lush greenery are synonymous with modernity and minimalism then conifers surely epitomise modern design. They are inherently non-flowering plants – in fact it is this characteristic that makes them what they are, botanically speaking. The foliage is usually green but can also be strikingly colourful in certain species, such as the golden Scots pine that turns yellow in the frost, or the blue cedar with a silvery colouration.

Finally, do not be fooled into thinking that the humble conifer has no use to man nor beast – barren as their reputation may be. Where would we be without the wonderful juniper? This conifer provides the flavour for gin as well as a smokeless fuel that was instrumental in the distilling of illegal whiskey to avoid detection by the taxman. And ***Ginkgo biloba*** – the maidenhair tree, is used as a cure for memory loss as well as having a beautiful, buttery yellow autumn colour and being the only conifer with fused needles that look like leaves. So there are many very compelling reasons for growing these underrated trees.

CEDRUS ATLANTICA GLAUCA

A few stunning examples of conifers are:

ATLAS CEDAR *(Cedrus atlantica)*

Available in both a blue-needled version and the traditional green, this glorious tree has an elegant habit and short, delicate needles arranged in whorls that look rather like sea urchins or something similar. Once it has reached full maturity this is a stunning and imposing specimen tree, complete with small purple fruits for a bit of added interest.

Height: 12 metres+
Spread: 8 metres+
Position: full sun
Hardiness: fully hardy

HIBA *(Thujopsis dolabrata)*

Unlike many conifers this tree has scales that are so large they could almost be mistaken for leaves. It is when you investigate the back of these scales that you will notice the pièce de résistance of this species – little white markings that look like angels' wings give a stunning adornment. This species is not upright or conical like many of its relatives but more sprawling and ever so slightly pendulous. It is endemic to Japan and has delicacy and elegance. A dwarf variety called 'Nana', which only reaches a height of 1m and spread of 80cm, can be used either in a container or in the ground in a smaller plot.

Height: 10–20m depending on climate
Spread: 5–10m depending on climate
Position: shade or partial sun
Hardiness: fully hardy

JAPANESE CEDAR
(Cryptomeria japonica)

This is another Japanese species of conifer that is truly stunning. To say that the foliage resembles oxygenation pond plants like elodea or hornwort may not sound like the best write up but, trust me, when you see the tree in all its glory you will see that this needle shape is almost unique to this genus and the effect is stunning. The similar foliage of *Taiwania* offers a similar shape to the Japanese cedar but with alarmingly spiky and vicious needles for keeping out unwanted visitors. If you have limited space, why not play on this plant's Japanese heritage and restrict its growth using bonsai methods and keep it in a container.

Height: up to 20m
Spread: up to 10m
Position: full sun
Hardiness: fully hardy

KOREAN FIR
(Abies koreana)

One characteristic almost unique to the conifer is the cone. There are all shapes and sizes of cone that can really enhance your garden, and when they drop they can go on to enhance your home. I have one given to me by a friend that I keep in pride of place because it is so very stunning. One conifer that will provide an abundance of beautiful cones is the Korean fir. With dusky blue/purple upright cones that eventually shed to look like candlesticks placed on the branch, this tree will make a statement. Unlike some other conifers this species is also quite slow growing so will take up to 50 years before it reaches its full height. This makes it more useful for a smaller garden, but do think long term and don't plant it in a tiny plot. This species cannot be pruned so be aware that once it does get too big it will need to be removed altogether. Having said that, for the years of joy that it will give it is well worth it.

It is a very architectural species with a perfectly conical shape and horizontal and flat branches with a uniform division habit. For those who like neatness, this may well be the conifer for you.

Height: 12m+
Spread: 4–8m
Position: full sun, neutral to acidic soil
Hardiness: fully hardy

HIBA (THUJOPSIS DOLABRATA)

SHRUBS

Like trees, shrubs are useful for adding structure, height and colour throughout the year and are grown for their attractive habit, foliage (deciduous or evergreen), flowers and fruit. They come in a wide variety of shapes and sizes so offer great variety and opportunity, both from a design and practical point of view. It's worth mentioning that shrubs can serve as a wonderful form of hedging (see pages 132–135), but for the purposes of this section we're thinking about shrubs as feature plants, either in the form of a solitary specimen or as part of an informal group in a border.

COTINUS COGGYGRIA 'ROYAL PURPLE'

When choosing a shrub, as well as considering its ornamental qualities think about its potential size and shape and its function. For instance, if you want to block a view or preserve your privacy, select an evergreen shrub that forms a dense canopy rather than a loosely branching deciduous species that loses its leaves in autumn. You also wouldn't want to plant a shrub that will only grow 30cm (12in) tall (and quite a few will) if you want to create a screen from your neighbours. For a shrub that will benefit wildlife, choose a species that produces flowers, seeds and fruit. It may seem like fairly obvious stuff, but it's all too easy to make mistakes if you don't think things through before planting.

SMOKE TREE
(Cotinus coggygria)

This is one of my favourite shrubs. Every time I see one, even now having seen so many, I am struck afresh by how stunning they are. One of the main reasons for this is the quality that they give to light. The leaves are round and translucent but with a matt or waxy quality unlike any other. When light shines through these leaves the colours produced are so rich that it is hard not to be impressed.

The smoke tree is a member of the same family as the cashew nut and though it does not produce any nuts, it does produce sprays of flowers reminiscent of smoke that gives the shrub its common name. These flowers then turn into fruits. The shrub comes in a variety of colours but the most common are green with a hint of soft blue, which is its natural form, or a deep purple. I cannot decide which I prefer, though the intense red autumn colour of the purple is breathtaking to behold, with a sort of rustic quality or appearance of oxidised copper.

The shrub can be grown either as a specimen or in conjunction with other shrubs and flowers to great effect.

Height: 4–8m
Spread: 4–8m
Position: sun or partial shade in any soil type
Hardiness: fully hardy

ELDER
(Sambucus nigra)

This is a beautiful shrub that can verge on being a tree but because it has foliage right to the base rather than a bare stem I am including it in with the shrubs.

I am a big fan of elder. It comes in the traditional green and also with deep purple foliage. Flat umbels of flowers appear in the spring (white flowers on the green elder and pink on the black) that can be eaten as fritters or turned into delicious cordial. These flowers then go on to become berries in the late summer. As berries go, elder berries are not the tastiest but this additional string to their bow does add visual interest as well as food for you, if you so desire, and, more importantly, for the birds.

I recommend 'Black Lace' as a particularly beautiful cultivar of elder.

Height: up to 8m
Spread: up to 5m
Position: full sun or partial shade in soil of any type, even salty coastal soils
Hardiness: fully hardy

SAMBUCUS NIGRA 'BLACK BEAUTY'

CHRISTMAS BOX
(Sarcococca hookeriana)

The wonderful thing about many shrubs is that they offer an evergreen alternative to conifers. Sarcococca provides year-round foliage as well as producing some of the most heavenly scents. The tiny white or pink flowers are borne just below the leaves in the depths of winter and the perfume can travel for metres, sometimes filling your whole garden with scent.

As its common name suggests, the foliage is reminiscent of box and can offer a less neat alternative to this hedging plant. Once the flowers have died away, it then goes on to produce black berries.

Confusa is very similar to *hookeriana* but some argue it has a sweeter smell and a slightly more compact habit.

Height: up to 1.5m
Spread: up to 2.5m
Position: full shade or partial shade in any soil
Hardiness: fully hardy

If the look of the Christmas box fails to get you excited but it sounds good on paper then have a look at the *Daphnes*, particularly *odora* or *bholua*. The scents of these shrubs will stop you in your tracks.

VIBURNUM SPP.

Again this is a slight cheat because the viburnum genus contains so many species that vary in size, habit and appearance. Some, like *V. tinus* and *V. davidii*, are evergreen with small, glossy leaves. *Tinus* will grow to up to 2.5m where the *davidii* is more likely to plateau at about 1–1.5m. They do not all have glossy foliage; the *rhytidophyllum* species have huge, hairy leaves with a dust-like orange under-surface. Some are deciduous, like the gelder rose (*Viburnum opulus*) famous for its pompom flowers, and *V. bodnantense* is more like a tree, which will bear heavily scented flowers on bare stems in the depths of winter and grows particularly

VIBURNUM TINUS

well in cities. Of the deciduous species, some have magnificent autumn colour.

One thing that all members of this genus do have in common is that every member produces sprays of flowers. Many of those flowers then go on to produce fruits of all colours. In some circumstances they are a fantastic choice for winter interest and in all circumstances they make for a fantastic ally in the garden.

I guarantee there is a viburnum out there for every position, soil type and purpose, and if nothing else, viburnums offer a little something for wildlife, be it shelter, pollen, nectar or berries.

SKIMMIA
(Skimmia japonica)

An evergreen shrub that offers winter interest, particularly in a shady position. The male is arguably more common and produces dense cones of purple, pink or white flowers in the winter. The female produces bright red, round berries (see page 20) that create a beautiful feature in the coldest months though are poisonous if ingested in any quantity so they are perhaps best avoided if you have children.

On both the male and female specimens the leaves are glossy, smooth and dark green in colour. This shrub is not a show-stopper, but it is dependable and fades into the background when other summer flowering species are taking centre stage then surprises you with its robust colour when you least expect it. For year-round form and structure, it is invaluable.

Height: 1–1.5m
Spread: 1–1.5m
Position: shade or partial sun in a neutral or acidic soil
Hardiness: fully hardy

EBBINGE'S SILVERBERRY
(Elaeagnus ebbingei)

I have to include this shrub simply because of its grit and fortitude. It is one of the most reliable shrubs and can basically take anything you can throw at it. Its tough, waxy leaves mean it can cope in intolerable heat without losing too much moisture and deal with wind and exposure as well as some degree of salt if you are near the sea. It is not showy and will never create a particularly impressive specimen but used in isolation in a modern design it will provide year-round greenery without being over fussy. The leaves have a silver underside and sometimes margins that give this shrub a little more aesthetic value than some other evergreen shrubs.

That said, the silverberry is by no means a shrinking violet. It will grow quickly and strongly to make its presence known. This may sound ominous but one of the main reasons for including this shrub is that it can cope with being pruned back to within an inch of its life and it will still throw up new stems reliably and quickly grow to fill its allotted space again. This is a plant that it is almost impossible to kill and that makes it worth using.

ELAEAGNUS EBBINGEI

Height: 2–4m
Spread: 2–4m
Position: full sun or partial shade in a well-drained soil of any type
Hardiness: fully hardy

SNOWY MESPILUS
(Amelanchier lamarckii)

There is some debate as to whether this is technically a tree or a large shrub. If you define a tree as single-stemmed and a shrub as multi-stemmed then this falls in the shrub section. It's a must-have as it works so very hard to earn its keep.

Delicate, white flowers that give the impression of snow on the branches (hence the name) are borne in the spring and then the oval leaves sit proud throughout summer. At the end of summer they turn a beautiful burnt orange or bronze before they fall from the tree. The delicate branches mean even in the depths of winter when there is not a leaf to be seen, it offers some architectural virtues.

Height: 8m+
Spread: 4m+
Position: sun or partial shade in any position with a neutral or acidic soil
Hardiness: fully hardy

RUSSIAN SAGE
(Perovskia spp.)

Tall, graceful spikes of blue flowers on almost white foliage are the distinguishing features of this plant. It can adorn a cottage-garden border or, if used in isolation or with a limited colour palette, can create a very modern effect.

Plant this sub-shrub in full sun and a free-draining soil.

LAVENDER
(Lavandula spp.)

With its lovely fragrant purple summer flowers and silver foliage, lavender is a great plant for hedging or as a single specimen. With regular deadheading it will flower right through to the first frosts and even beyond on occasion.

This short lived sub-shrub will need pruning back – never into the old wood but only to where it is green in late summer or spring and will need a sunny, free-draining position although it is fully hardy. It will never reach heights of more than a metre.

HEDGING PLANTS

A timeless feature of the garden, hedges are inherently practical but often beautiful, too. They act as boundaries and dividers, sometimes to screen unsightly areas of the garden.

Some dwarf hedging plants, such as lavender, can be kept small by clipping and used to edge a path, flowerbed or formal herb garden.

Although hedges are often associated with traditional-style gardens, they can also be chic and modern. A variety of hedges used cleverly throughout the garden either as border edges, around buildings, along the perimeter or to interrupt your view along the plot can add height and interest in your garden in a dynamic, contemporary way, eliminating the need to build hard structures. And consider using unconventional hedging plants – for instance, reeds or even sweetcorn can create a screen that has movement or produces a crop.

Hedges are wonderful for wildlife. For maximum biodiversity, plant a mixed hedge consisting of several species of native plants, like the traditional hedgerows found in the countryside. However, a hedge of any kind is better for the environment than a fence, so even if you opt for a classic hedge of one species alone you'll be making a difference.

Hedging options

Plants for hedging are generally trees or shrubs, but it's vital to select the right kinds. They must not grow too tall and they must be able to be pruned – heavily so if required. Ideally, they will also let some light through. A hedge that is too tall or dense can end up blocking your light and taking all the available moisture from the soil, effectively turning your garden into a barren space.

Traditionally, conifers have been a favourite for hedges and there are some, such as yew (*Taxus baccata*, see page 135), that are ideal. However, sadly there are many that are planted that are not suitable, mainly because very few conifers should be pruned; if you cut into last year's wood, they won't recover. The upshot is that they get bigger and bigger as each year passes until you have something huge and overbearing. Think of the Leyland cypress (*Cuprocyparis leylandii*), which is used over and over again as a hedge even though it's totally unsuitable. It's incredibly fast growing and therefore it can be something of a brute. Its foliage is so dense that no light at all is allowed through, and it takes all the water from the soil beneath it. Worst of all, when you give it a hard prune to keep its size in check it turns brown and will frequently turn up its toes and die.

Here are some plants that can be used successfully for hedging:

BOX
(Buxus sempervirens)

A box hedge is evergreen and incredibly versatile – it can be kept as low as 30cm (12in) or grown to around 1.4m (4.5ft) or just a little taller, and left a little shaggy, with a flush of electric-green foliage if its new growth is left a little longer, or clipped to a pristine finish. It even makes a stunning tree if left unclipped. Single specimens, clipped into topiary balls, pillars, pyramids or any other shape you can think of, can also be lined up and used to make a very formal and artistic hedge. Dwarf box hedges take a very long time to grow but you have the guarantee that they will never get too big. But as you can cut back as hard as you like into normal box, if you are looking for a hedge to establish quickly this is probably the best option.

As for maintenance, box requires very little care. It's not fussy about its soil type and needs only one clip a year, usually in late spring, to keep it in check. If you want a formal or pristine finish, clipping can be repeated until late autumn. It can also be pruned back very heavily if required.

The only potential problem with this species is that it is susceptible to a disease called box blight. If it contracts this it will turn brown or red and will quite quickly die. Although this problem is not incredibly common, it's worth doing a little detective work before spending a lot of money on a box hedge. If anyone living nearby has had their plant affected by this disease, consider an alternative such as box-leaved holly (*Ilex crenata*).

BOX CLIPPED TOPIARY HEDGE

PRIVET
(Ligustrum ovalifolium)

Privet makes a wonderful evergreen hedge. Most commonly the foliage is a mid-green with small, oval leaves, but it can also be golden or even variegated. It will grow in most soil types and will form a dense hedge of some size, if required, without dominating or casting impenetrable shade as some conifers tend to do.

Incidentally, this species is great for feeding the dreaded stick insects. It is not as great for humans, though so beware its black berries, which are slightly toxic and although they are more likely to cause a stomach upset than anything worse they are best kept away from children. You can prune them off and a hedge that is regularly clipped will tend not to have many, if any, berries.

HAWTHORN
(Crataegus monogyna)

The hawthorn, or mayflower, is a fantastic all-rounder and must be included for the simple reason that it serves the function of helping to prevent unwanted guests entering your garden. That may sound brutal and a little misanthropic, but protecting your boundaries is and has always been a prime reason for planting a hedge in the first place. And that's not to say that this hedge will exclude all visitors – its blossom in late spring and berries in late summer invite all sorts of wildlife into your garden. But the thorns, which can measure up to 4cm (1.5in) long, will act as a deterrent to intruders.

Apart from its practical function, hawthorn makes a beautiful hedge. Oak-shaped deciduous foliage comes out as the blossom emerges, then red berries follow, looking stunning against the bright green of the foliage. These berries feed the birds and can also be dried and used as decoration – especially for Christmas. It will never make the neatest hedge, but its unruly character is part of what I love about it. It evokes the countryside in spring and the scent that comes from its blossoms is heady and sweet.

A clip in early summer and again in early autumn will keep this species from getting too big for its allocated space.

HAWTHORN (CRATAGEUS MONOGYNA)

BLACKTHORN
(Prunus spinosa)

This is another species that acts as a wonderful barrier that will put both creatures and people off attempting entry into your property because of its impressive thorns. Commonly known as the sloe berry bush, blackthorn is a lovely deciduous hedge with small, dark green leaves, delicate blossom in the spring and juicy (though unimaginably sour) berries in the autumn that are famously used to flavour sloe gin. This species will also encourage birds and insects so it's a great choice if you want to bring in wildlife.

HOLLY (ILEX AQUIFOLIUM)

HOLLY
(Ilex spp.)

Yet another spiky customer, though holly spikes are found on the leaves rather than thorny stems. Never fear, though, as holly does not lose its foliage over the winter so you will still have year-round protection.

The lovely thing about holly is that it comes in all kinds of different colours. Traditional holly is a dark, glossy green with red berries, if you have a female specimen (the males will not produce berries). There are, however, lots of other species that offer myriad variations. There are hollies with different stem colours and all styles and colours of variegation. Interestingly you can often tell a holly's gender based on its name but not in quite the way you would expect. Traditionally hollies are given names of the opposite sex. 'Silver Milkboy', for example, is a lovely female holly with leaves that have pale yellow variegation. 'Silver Queen' is a male holly, which also has attractive variegation but does not produce berries. Some hollies are not given a gender specific name, in which case you will need to do further investigation if you specifically want berries. And it is well worth the investigation.

TAXUS BACCATA 'FASTIGIATA AUREA'

YEW
(Taxus baccata)

Steeped in history and mystery, yew is one of the only conifers that can be pruned as much as you like. It does exclude a lot of light and needs plenty of water, but it makes a fantastic evergreen hedge.

Yews are either male or female. The male has small yellow/brown flowers whereas the female produces big red berries otherwise known as snot berries because they are full of a clear goo.

The plant has dark glossy foliage with delicate oppositely arranged needles. Golden yew offers an alternative with brighter, paler foliage. And if you really hate maintenance, the fastigiate yew has a naturally upright growth so needs a little less clipping on the sides.

Mazes, topiary and Italianate-style gardens all feature clipped yew, so if you like that formal look, this is for you. Yews are highly poisonous – the berries aren't, but the seeds inside them are, and the rest of the plant is also toxic, so they are best avoided if you have children. Trim in late summer and neaten when required.

BEECH
(Fagus sylvatica)

This is the classic choice of hedge for many gardeners, and with good reason. It isn't evergreen, but it does retain its leaves for most of the winter – although they will turn brown. These leaves will then be shed in early spring and replaced with zingy, papery, slightly crimped-looking foliage of intense green. The effect is simply stunning, and that alone makes this a worthwhile species to choose for a hedge.

Beech is extremely versatile and can grow to about 30m (100ft) high but still be kept just a metre or so wide. To grow a hedge of such proportions will take decades, if not centuries, but nonetheless beech can create dramatic boundaries without casting too much shade through its delicate, translucent foliage. It can be pruned to shape and kept small. The best time for cutting back is in late summer.

CHERRY LAUREL
(Prunus laurocerasus)

This is one of my favourite hedging plants. It has beautiful, abundant broad leaves that are bright green and glossy all year round, guaranteeing you a perpetually cheerful hedge. It is not too dense either, and although a fully grown specimen will not let an awful lot of light through, it is still far less impenetrable than any conifer. Laurel produces an informal, leafy hedge rather than a formal, neat one. This is because the large leaves can't be clipped with shears without cutting them in half, which would make them turn brown at the edges, so the overall effect of a laurel hedge is free and a little unruly.

Another feature of this species is that it produces some rather lovely, feathery flower spikes followed by stunning, perfectly round, almost-black fruits. So this hedge gives you every bit of interest you could want and also provides shelter and a food source for wildlife, especially birds.

One clip in early summer and another in early autumn should keep this hedge looking neat and tidy. To avoid damage to the leaves, use secateurs rather than shears and cut below the leaf rather than through it. If the plant becomes too big, prune it back hard in early spring.

Incidentally, laurel will not cope in salty conditions, so if you have a seaside garden and need a hedge as a form of shelter from salty winds, an alternative hedging shrub is *Griselinia littoralis*. It is very similar in habit to laurel, with big, waxy, bright green leaves all year round, but can cope with very salty conditions. A word of warning – this plant will seed itself prolifically, so be vigilant with weeding at its base.

BAMBOO

If you really haven't got the energy for a hedge but would still like some vegetation to cover your boundaries then consider a bamboo or reed, or even a robust grass. Bamboos need fairly moist soil but grow well in most soils. They have striking stems, often green but also in gold or deep purple/black, and delicate foliage. They may need planting in a concrete-lined trench to stop the runners from spreading through the ground and popping up over the garden (and the neighbours') but other than that they really do not need any maintenance at all.

BAMBOO SCREENING

THE PROS & CONS OF HEDGING

PROS

- Hedges allow wind to pass through the gaps, whereas a fence can cause such an abrupt barrier to the wind that it can either create a vortex that increases the wind's force in the garden, or the first gusts will knock down the fence and cause extensive damage to the garden or even the property. A hedge will filter the wind, avoiding both of these risks.

- Hedges make aesthetically pleasing boundaries and allow you to have a changing perimeter throughout the year – with some clever choices.

- In limited space or a garden that needs to be low maintenance, a hedge can act as the main plant interest in the garden without infringing too much on the plot, allowing room for other features.

- Hedges can be a very cheap method of creating a boundary if you buy small specimens, saplings or whips to create them.

- Using a spiky or thorny hedge like a holly or a hawthorn can be a real deterrent for neighbours' pets or even intruders.

- Once a hedge is there that's it. You may need to prune it every year but there are no preserving treatments required (as with fencing) and it will not need replacing after a few years.

- Hedging can offer all kinds of interest such as bringing in scents and colour.

- Hedges are good for the environment. Birds, bees, butterflies and all manner of creatures find somewhere to shelter, nest, roost and feed within them.

CONS

- Hedging is less secure than a fence. If you have small, exploratory children and a garden that backs onto a road, or the neighbour has a greyhound and you have a rabbit, a solid barrier such as a wall or fence is preferable.

- A hedge can be an expensive option if you use mature specimens.

- For those who like order, a hedge can be a little scruffy – especially if it goes unpruned.

- Hedges take up nutrients from the soil, giving you slightly less options of plants to grow against them in the dry shade provided by them than if using a fence.

- Fencing is much faster to put up than a hedge is to grow.

CLIMBERS

Although valuable in all gardens, climbing plants are particularly useful for those with very limited space. They can break up stark expanses of walls and fences and soften the hard lines of fencing or trellis, creating the impression of a hedge without taking up as much room. And a climber growing vertically up a post or obelisk can be used as a tree substitute to create height and a focal point in an otherwise two-dimensional display.

WHITE CLIMBING ROSE

Climbers can be used to disguise or obscure eyesores and bring a splash of colour and variety to dull areas of the garden by planting through lacklustre trees and shrubs, allowing you to squeeze even more plants into a restricted area. Some climbers can become very large, but most can be cut back if they outgrow their space.

Climbers produce glorious displays of flowers, fruits and foliage, and can also provide a good food source. Take the passionflower (*Passiflora*) for example, which has breathtakingly stunning blooms that turn into delicious, healthy fruits. There are also grapevines that are incredibly easy to grow and annual climbing beans and peas that add colour as well as provide food. And consider the humble hop (*Humulus lupulus*). This plant is becoming more and more popular as a climber in domestic gardens. Not only does it grow from the ground each year into a beautiful, big climber, but it fills your garden with its musky, hoppy scent, provides great food for insects – particularly butterflies – makes a great decoration in your home when it's dried and can be used to brew your own beer. What more could anybody ask for?

Climbing and rambler roses

For those who love tradition and want to create a cottage-garden look, a climbing or rambler rose is a must. There are numerous rose varieties that are specifically designed to climb, although they all need a helping hand in the form of a support and regular tying in. These roses are divided into two types: climbing and rambler roses. Their main flowering time is early summer, but many flower more than once in a season or almost continuously through summer and into autumn. They're often highly fragrant, and some produce colourful hips (berries) that provide food for wildlife.

In general, ramblers tend to be bigger and more vigorous than climbing roses, so if you like the rather wild, unruly look, and are seeking a rose to grow through a tree or up a pergola, for instance, a rambler might be the choice for you. 'Kew Rambler', 'Kiftsgate', 'Blush Rambler', 'Rambling Rector' and 'Tea Rambler' are just a few recommended varieties.

If you have a smaller space to fill, or would prefer something a little less boisterous – perhaps you want to grow a rose around an arch or doorway, or up a wall – you may prefer a climbing rose. 'Étoile de Hollande' is a personal favourite of mine, with deep red flowers and a heavenly scent, but there are all sorts in a variety of colours. For pinks, try 'Fashion Climber', 'Lady Sylvia', 'Constance Spry' or 'Ballerina'. If you prefer white roses, look at 'Madame Alfred Carrière', 'Niphetos' or 'Iceberg', or if you prefer yellows you could try 'Lady Hillingdon', 'Golden Showers' or 'Golden Future'. And if you prefer subtle shades of peach, have a look at 'Masquerade' or 'Mrs Sam McGredy'.

And as well as a choice of colour you can even choose to have thornless varieties, such as 'Zéphirine Drouhin' or 'A Shropshire Lad' (though these will need additional assistance in climbing), and varieties that are resistant to the dreaded black spot that roses suffer from so frequently, for instance 'Debutante'. Black spot will not actually kill a rose, it will just cause the leaves to yellow and fall, so is disfiguring, but as long as you make sure you remove all the foliage from the ground each autumn you'll keep it to a minimum.

SPECIES ROSES

Most roses that we grow are the result of centuries of extensive breeding and cultivation to produce the most ornate, multi-petalled or highly fragrant blooms. However, there is a revival of interest in what are known as species roses, such as *Rosa rugosa* (the beach or saltspray rose) or *Rosa canina* (the dog rose). Of these two, the dog rose is probably more commonly used as a climber whereas the beach rose, although it will scramble to some extent, is commonly planted en masse to create hedgerows or even kept clipped in containers.

Species roses are very similar to their wild rose ancestors and retain their basic characteristics – single flowers produced in one flush in early summer, followed by large, brightly coloured hips. As well as being very attractive, species roses have the advantage of being excellent for wildlife. Bees and other pollinating insects can easily access the nectar and pollen from the flowers' centres, and birds love the hips.

PINK SHRUB ROSE

CLIMBING METHODS

Plants climb in a number of ways. It's important to understand the climbing methods of the specific plants you choose so that you can put them in a suitable position and provide the correct support where necessary.

AERIAL ROOTS along the plant's stems work their way into tiny crevices in the stone or brick of a wall or the bark of a tree. Ivy and climbing hydrangea both climb this way.

TENDRILS with sticky pads on the end are produced on some climbers, for instance Virginia creeper (*Parthenocissus quinquefolia*). The pads 'cement' the climber to any surface.

TWINING CLIMBERS such as morning glory (*Ipomoea*), passionflower (*Passiflora*), honeysuckle (*Lonicera*), wisteria and runner beans, have stems or twisting tendrils that wrap around their host. In the garden you will need to provide an artificial support.

THORNS on the stems of plants such as climbing roses hook themselves onto their host. Plants that climb this way need trellis for support and tying in as they grow to keep them secure.

IVY (HEDERA)

CLIMBING BEAN

GRAPEVINE (VITIS)

WISTERIA

Other climbers

There are plenty of other climbers that are suitable for the first-time gardener, offering beautiful flowers and foliage, and some providing autumn colour or berries.

CLEMATIS
(Clematis spp.)

This is a varied and rather complicated group of climbers, all with slightly different requirements and needing specific pruning treatments. There are a few species that are easier for the first-time gardener and require minimum upkeep with maximum results, such as *Clematis montana* and *Clematis armandii.* Like all clematis, they require their roots to be in shade while their stems are in sun. An upturned flowerpot or small pile of stones at their base will provide adequate shade for the roots.

Clematis montana is a vigorous form that will grow tall and take over fences, hedges and walls and grow stunning flowers ranging from purple through pink to white. Those flowers turn to beautiful seed heads throughout the winter. Prune by cutting it back as much as required immediately after flowering.

Clematis armandii can be pruned in exactly the same way. This clematis will grow in a similar way to the *montana* in that it will take over most surfaces and can be cut to its base if it gets too vigorous and contains too much dead wood. The *armandii* clematis has many evergreen varieties though, making it potentially more versatile, especially in a small garden. The flowers are similarly elegant and come in almost identical colours.

CLEMATIS SPP.

CLIMBING HYDRANGEA
(Hydrangea petiolaris)

I have included this because it is one of the only climbers that will grow on a north-facing wall. Another is winter-flowering jasmine (*Jasminum nudiflorum*). As well being useful for growing against cold, shady walls, the climbing hydrangea is a stunning plant, with delicate white flowers in late spring and early summer and contrasting, glossy dark green leaves.

It has a tendency to become quite large and heavy, so train it against a sturdy brick wall with plenty of space around. Don't plant it where it can obscure light coming into windows because the dense foliage will block a lot of light. Use vine-eyes and wire to really secure it to the wall otherwise it can fall forwards. Vine-eyes and wire are also a really good way of controlling a climber's growth by using the wiring as a framework to which the climber can be cut back, keeping it in check.

Prune hydrangea quite quickly after it has flowered, as the new flower buds are formed quite soon after the current season's flowers have gone over, and if you cut off stems with new buds you'll have fewer flowers next year. Otherwise, this is very low maintenance and can cope with all sorts of tough conditions.

HONEYSUCKLE
(Lonicera spp.)

I love honeysuckle. There is something very simple and giving about honeysuckle – it is unpretentious and incredibly pretty.

Honeysuckle serves much the same function as many clematis species as it will quickly scramble up a wall and produce prolific flowers but I prefer it for two reasons. The first is that it smells absolutely delicious, the second is that it tastes absolutely delicious. I urge you to taste it next time you see one in flower (though don't forget to leave some for the bees). Break off one of the long, tubular flowers as near to the base as possible and suck out the nectar from the bottom end. It's incredibly tasty.

You can cut honeysuckle back as much as you like in early spring. A lot of dead, woody material tends to accumulate beneath the new growth and if left unchecked this can become a real eyesore, so remove all of this and the honeysuckle will look brand new. Otherwise, just neaten up any very long shoots as they appear and remove any dead ones. If you want to regenerate the plant, hack it back to no less than 60cm (24in) in early spring.

With the evergreen forms of climbing honeysuckle, you will need to do very little pruning. Merely cut the plant back where it has become too long. A common and popular variety of honeysuckle is *L. periclymenum* and unlike most species it flowers on older wood. As a consequence this should only ever be pruned immediately after it has finished flowering in order to guarantee flowers next year.

Honeysuckle is not fussy about soil type but it will do especially well in a humus-rich position and flower more prolifically if the tips are in full sun.

JASMINE
(Jasminum officinale)

Jasmine is a perennially popular choice of flowering climber. Like honeysuckle it has a scent that is heady but the flowers of a jasmine are pure white and star-like.

It may take a few years for a jasmine to take off but once it has it will grow quickly and spread great distances. The leaves are compound and delicate and golden varieties are available. It is the flowers of this plant that, rather obviously, give the flavour to jasmine tea.

This climber can grow in any soil type in sun or partial shade and will reach eventual heights to up to 8m (26ft) and a spread of up to 2.5m (18ft).

CHINESE VIRGINIA CREEPER (*Parthenocissus henryana*)

Virginia creeper (*P. quinquefolia*) has a terrible reputation, being notorious for taking over a house or wall. Personally, I much prefer man-made structures to be covered by plants, but I realise not everyone feels the same way. Also, a climber can damage brickwork and guttering on a property so if you are worried about damage it is always safer to go for something less vigorous. That is why I have decided to recommend the Chinese Virginia creeper (*P. henryana*) in preference to the traditional Virginia creeper. Being less rampant – Virginia creeper's mild-mannered little brother – it will not grow extensively in temperate regions but will fill out a space and really beautify a wall, fence or post. The leaves of this species are also more attractive than those of the plain Virginia creeper, ranging from a bluish green to purple, silver and red – with all of those colours in just one leaf.

This climber really comes into its own in autumn, when the leaves turn the most stunning shade of scarlet. They will then drop off, leaving rather unprepossessing bare stems throughout the winter months.

IVY (*Hedera spp.*)

If you prefer an evergreen option that will quickly cover any hard landscape features that you want obscured, you might be better off with an ivy.

LATE SUMMER IVY FLOWERS

These plants have a slightly bad reputation as brutes. On a house ivy can cause some damage to roof tiles, brick mortar, guttering and even window frames, but the truth is that there are many varieties of ivy that are far less vigorous and actually extremely attractive. Variegated forms are particularly beautiful.

The lovely thing about ivy is that it will grow on any surface including wood, even trees, as well as fences and trellising, wire, stone and brick. It also provides invaluable food for bees as it flowers at the end of the season when most other plants have gone to seed.

The eventual size of ivy can be almost indeterminate but more specialist species will be smaller. No ivy is fussy about its soil type, though you might find more healthy-looking growth occurs in the shade or partial sun.

WISTERIA (*Wisteria spp.*)

How could I not include a wisteria in my shortlist? There is nothing more beautiful than one of these awe-inspiring plants in full flower adorning the front of someone's home. They are simply majestic. And even without flowers, the thick, corkscrew trunks and delicate foliage are something to behold. Both Chinese wisteria (*Wisteria sinensis*) and Japanese (*Wisteria floribunda*) are popular in gardens the world over. The Chinese plant might be slightly more commonly used with shorter, more generous flowers ranging from purple to white, but the Japanese wisteria has flowers of extreme length (sometimes up to 50cm (20in) long) which are equally beguiling.

There are two things to be aware of when choosing a wisteria. The first is that they can take a long time to reach maturity and start flowering. Make sure you buy one that has been grafted and is already at flowering age, or you might find yourself waiting for anything up to 20 years for your first flower. The second thing to be aware of is that there is a quite specific regime that needs to be carried out in order to keep these climbers in check and looking their best. Don't be daunted, though – even the most inexperienced gardener can manage it. You'll need to prune in two stages (see box, opposite). In addition, give the climber a high potassium feed in spring and be sure to water the plant in times of drought.

WISTERIA ON AN ARCH

HOW TO PRUNE WISTERIA

In late summer, after your wisteria has flowered, cut the long, whippy stems of the current season's growth back to six buds. Then, in mid- to late winter, cut those same stems back to two buds. There will be no leaves at this time of year to gauge this by, but you will clearly see where the buds will form, as the stems in those places will be swollen. You may find that after your summer prune, particularly in an Indian summer, there will be excessive regrowth of the shoots. In such cases it is fine to cut those shoots back as required as long as you make sure you do not take the growth back to less than six buds and preferably no shorter than 20cm (8in).

PERENNIALS

The wonderful thing about perennials is that they come back year after year, provided they're planted in the right position. They are the largest group of hardy garden plants and also the most versatile, with varieties to suit every situation and garden style and spanning all seasons. The flowers of some perennials can be every bit as big and showy as their annual cousins, and the leaves of many make stunning displays in their own right.

ASTRANTIA MAJOR

Recommended perennials

One really good tip is that you should make a monthly trip to a garden centre and look at whatever plants are in flower, buy the ones you like and then you will have guaranteed flowers all year. The problem with impulse buying like this is that you can never be sure that the plants you choose will be happy in the spot you have in mind. But there are a few visual clues that show you a plant's preferred position if you know how to spot them.

The plants that follow are just a tiny selection of plants from this huge group. I have chosen a few of my favourites as well as a few that are easy to grow and make a big impact. Try to get maximum colour in your space throughout the year by either choosing plants that look good for a long time or by succession planting, which is where one flower takes over when another one ends. Once you've tried growing these, I'm sure you'll want to experiment with more.

AFRICAN LILY (*Agapanthus spp.*)

This South African flower has become an international favourite in recent years, as it's so versatile. Like an allium, *agapanthus* flowerheads are perfectly spherical. But rather than being purple, they are bright blue – a colour that is hard to come by in the natural world and which makes it a striking addition to any garden. They flower late (usually late summer), so will add a splash of colour when a lot of other plants might be going over. Some varieties of *agapanthus* are evergreen and provide grass-like foliage throughout the year.

Agapanthus can look great combined with other plants, for instance in a cottage-garden scheme, augmenting the display without overpowering it. If planted en masse, as has been done by some influential designers in recent years, the effect is strikingly modern.

In terms of care, *agapanthus* needs a dryish position, particularly somewhere that won't get wet for long periods during winter. Most *agapanthus* are fully hardy, so there's no need to worry too much about frosts; a good mulch in the winter should see them safely through the coldest weather. Some though, particularly the evergreen varieties, can be tender so will either need a bit of protection, again as a mulch, with straw or fleece, or lifting and placing in a cold frame or greenhouse until the spring. You can also grow *agapanthus* in pots; they respond well to having their roots restricted.

DYER'S CHAMOMILE (*Anthemis tinctoria*)

Bees and other pollinating insects adore the yellow, daisy-like flowers of this plant, but the reason I have included it is that it also possesses some very beautiful silvery foliage. Wherever possible, I try to select plants that have more than one purpose, and to have attractive foliage as well as flowers is always an added bonus. This plant could not be easier to grow and will thrive in any sunny position and well-drained soil. Depending on the cultivar, the flowers come in a variety of yellows, from pale primrose to deep mustard, or may be white with a yellow centre. Another plant that would serve a similar function, with a dense clump of fine, scented, silver foliage, but with smaller flowers, is the silver mound mugwort (*Artemisia schmidtiana*). With both of these plants, the foliage can be trimmed back with shears and the flowers will just keep coming all through the summer.

DYER'S CHAMOMILE

CONE FLOWER (ECHINACEA PURPUREA)

CONE FLOWER (*Echinacea purpurea*)

This stunning flower ranges from deep pink through to white. The petals are long and thin and are perfectly horizontal or hang slightly down. But these petals, though they are beautiful, are not the main show-stopper of this plant. The defining characteristic and the feature that gives it its name is the spiny, cone-shaped disc in the centre of the flowerhead. It makes for a very striking addition to the garden.

Traditionally, this plant has been used as a tincture to cure colds. So the flower is functional as well as beautiful, and the bees and butterflies love them, too. Unfortunately, so do slugs and snails, so you may need to put down a deterrent, especially when the shoots first break through in spring.

ERYSIMUM 'BOWLES MAUVE'

PERENNIAL WALLFLOWER *(Erysimum spp.)*

As this plant's name indicates, it will grow in a wall, but it can also grow in a border and can be clipped into a hedge. It has delicate, bluish-green foliage combined with flowers that were traditionally purple but now come in yellows and burnt oranges. It is fantastic for bees, and if planted in any number you'll hear bees buzzing around them all summer long.

This is not to be confused with the traditional wallflower so often used as a bedding plant. The bedding wallflower is a biennial. You plant the young plant in the autumn and it flowers at the start of the following season. The bedding wallflower is heavily scented, especially when planted en masse and will make a great display, but unlike its perennial sister, it will not come back again once flowering has finished, but will set seed and die, meaning it needs replacing annually. This is well worth the effort if you have the time.

BABY'S BREATH *(Gypsophila spp.)*

The exquisitely dainty, white or pink flowers of baby's breath create a mist-like effect in a border, especially in the early morning. They may be single or double-flowered. If you're keen on flower arranging and cut flowers, these are a must-have. The softening effect they have in a border can also create texture and blend planting schemes in a way that even the most inexperienced gardener can master.

MASTERWORT *(Astrantia major)*

This is a plant that you need to see up close and touch to really appreciate. It has beguiling white/green, purple or pink flowers about 3–5cm (1.25–2in) in diameter, with pointy petals and a breathtaking crown of elaborate stamens and stigmas. The petal points are tipped with green and veined, and feel like rough paper.

Maintenance is easy with a hack back once the flowers have finished and it will cope in most moisture-retentive but free-draining soils.

HELLEBORES or CHRISTMAS ROSE *(Helleborus niger)*

This is a great perennial plant for two reasons. First, it is one of the first flowers in the garden, so for early colour it is invaluable. Secondly, it will cope very well with intense shade. The flowers are cup-shaped and range from white to deep purple. A lot of people remove the leaves once the plant starts flowering, but I prefer to leave them on as it is better for the plant and I like the foliage. The messier leaves can be snipped off and always remove any foliage that may be diseased. If you want to try a hellebore with attractive foliage then look at *Helleborus foetidus*.

SIBERIAN IRIS *(Iris sibirica)*

The Siberian iris has lovely, delicate, intense blue or purple flowers (though it can come in more varied colours now) on fine stems that are hidden by a mass of grass-like foliage. It is such a lovely, delicate iris and can fit into modern or classic schemes, depending on what is planted around it. Siberian irises flower in the spring, and when they have gone over the foliage gradually turns a beautiful bronze colour. Cut them back each autumn and they will come back again and again.

If you like the flower but not the foliage, try a bearded iris. It comes in a wider variety of colours and has silver, strappy or linear leaves. Some of these flowers such as 'White Knight' and 'Autumn Tryst' are even delicately scented. Make sure if you plant these that they are in a hot, dry place and that the big rhizomes (or thick surface roots) are just above the surface of the soil so that the sun can bake them. That way they will produce flowers.

CATMINT *(Nepeta spp.)*

This silver-leaved, purple-flowered plant is indispensable in a sunny border. Cut it back a few times a year into a mound and the flowers will keep coming all summer. The leaves not only look lovely, they're scented too – a double whammy.

CATMINT (NEPETA)

LAMB'S EARS (STACHYS BYZANTINA)

LAMB'S EARS
(Stachys byzantina)

Although grown mainly for its soft, downy silver foliage that spreads along the ground, lamb's ears also produces spikes of purple flowers for a short period in early summer. It's a great plant to grow at the front of a border and fantastic for kids, who love to stroke it.

ORIENTAL POPPY
(Papaver orientale)

A cheerful addition to the flower garden, this poppy generally comes in shades of red and orange, but there are some lovely purple- and peach-coloured cultivars like 'Patty's Plum', 'Marlene' and 'Salmon Glow' that create a different feel. The flowers are always big and bold, and the petals are papery and thin. Once the flowers have gone over, cut the whole plant back almost to the ground with shears and it will produce a lovely rosette of foliage, so even when not in flower it still makes a welcome addition of greenery to your outside space.

VALERIAN
(Valeriana officinalis)

I have to include valerian because it will grow in almost any soil type and position, including walls, damp areas beside a pond and near the coast. In addition, with its reddish-pink, pale pink or white flowers, it's stunning and will create a very natural effect within a planting scheme. It tends to seed itself here, there and everywhere, but as a plant that will grow in places where not much else will survive, this can be a real advantage. Bees love it, too.

RED HOT POKER
(Kniphofia spp.)

Red hot pokers are great plants to grow because they make such a striking feature from the height of summer right through to the first frosts. They have a clump of strappy foliage that can survive all year if the frost does not hit it too hard, and if it does get frost damage, you can cut it back to a few inches and wait for it to return again the following year. The flowers are spikes of red, orange, yellow, cream or green, formed on thick, fleshy stems that tower above the plant's foliage.

They are great for wildlife, easy to grow and will thrive in most conditions, even coastal, as long as they don't get too wet.

BLUE VERVAIN
(Verbena bonariensis)

There are many good reasons why this perennial is so popular. It starts flowering in mid- to late summer and keeps going through the autumn to the end of the growing season. The tiny flowers are borne on tall stems, and they are invaluable for providing height without bulk, giving them a 'see-through' quality. The plants work fantastically well in traditional planting schemes, but they also make a real statement in a modern design and are great for cutting and dried flowers.

The prairie planting trend that has become very popular in recent years relies heavily on *Verbena bonariensis*, as it looks particularly stunning with grasses.

RED HOT POKER (KNIPHOFIA)

VERBENA BONARIENSIS

ARUM LILY OR CALLA
(Zantedeschia aethiopica)

Traditionally, this elegant plant existed only in white forms, but in recent years plant breeders have bred a variety of interesting colours, including yellow, orange, red, pink, purple, black and green with a dark centre. The leaves are big and arrow-shaped and the flowers are like a curled piece of paper. Arum lilies can be damaged by frost, so protect them in extreme cold, and do not plant them in direct sun. They need a little shade for protection. If you have success with these plants, you will fall head over-heels in love with them.

PLANTS FOR WILDLIFE

In any wildlife garden one of the most important components is water. It can be a pond, a bowl or a birdbath. But water, preferably containing some plants, offers a home for the pupal stage of many insects, for amphibious animals and somewhere to drink and clean for all kinds of animals.

When selecting plants to encourage wildlife, include plenty of colourful or fragrant flowers to attract insect pollinators. Wherever possible, select species with single flowers, as they allow insects to collect pollen and nectar. Double-flowered species have replaced their reproductive parts with more petals and are therefore sterile, so they cannot be pollinated and won't produce fruits or seeds, which are beloved by birds and insects.

Some people seem to think that wildlife needs native species. While it is true that some native plants support a wider range of species (for instance certain native wildflowers and trees), you will attract plenty of wildlife to the garden if you choose wildlife-friendly plants with the features described above, regardless of their origin. For more information, see page 42.

Here are some plants that are invaluable for wildlife:

COTONEASTER

HAWTHORN (CRATAEGUS)

PYRACANTHA

REDCURRANT (RIBES)

TREES AND SHRUBS

Buddleia (*Buddleja*)
Pyracantha
Apple and Crab apple (*Malus spp.*)
Cherry, plum, damson and blackthorn (*Prunus spp.*)
Roses – particularly ones that form hips (*Rosa spp.*)
Hawthorn (*Crataegus spp.*)
Rowan (*Sorbus spp.*)
Holly (*Ilex aquifolium*)
Hazel (*Corylus avellana*)
Cotoneaster
Birch (*Betula spp.*)
Blueberry and cranberry (*Vaccinium spp.*)
Poplar (*Populus spp.*)
Elder (*Sambucus nigra*)
Lavender (*Lavendula spp.*)

BIENNIALS

Foxglove (*Digitalis spp.*)
Echium
Honesty

HONESTY SEEDS (LUNARIA ANNUA)

FERNS

OTHER

Mosses and ferns

PERENNIALS

Hollyhock (*Alcea*)
Torch lily (*Kniphofia*)
Valerian (*Valeriana*)
Wallflower (*Erysimum*)
Sea holly (*Eryngium*)
Alium
Crocus
Veronicastrum
Ornamental sage (*Salvia*)
Cow parsley (*Anthriscus*)
Angelica
Lobelia
Dead nettles (*Lamium*)

RED DEAD NETTLE (LAMIUM)

ORNAMENTAL SAGE (SALVIA)

HOLLYHOCK (ALCEA)

ANNUALS

Borage
Nasturtium
Marigold
Annual poppy
Opium poppy
Sweet pea
Edible beans
Edible peas
Sunflower
Nigella

EDIBLE PEA

CLIMBERS

Ivy (*Hedera spp.*)
Hops (*Humulus lupulus*)
Honeysuckle (*Lonicera spp.*)
Jasmine (*Jasminum spp.*)
Passionflower
(*Passiflora spp.*)

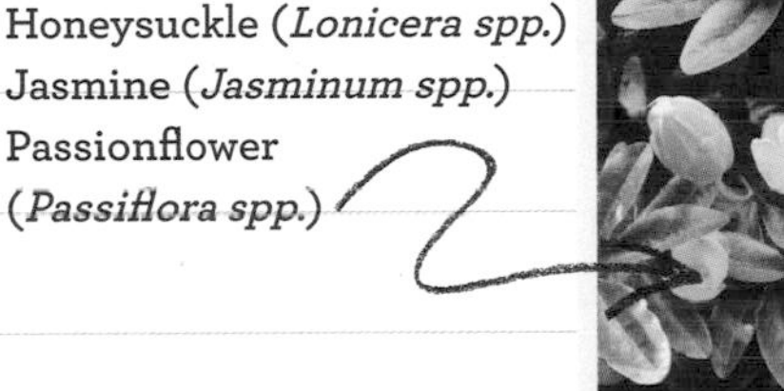

PASSIONFLOWER (PASSIFLORA)

SUNFLOWER

BORAGE

NASTURTIUM

EDIBLE BEAN

ANNUALS

The mainstay of summer bedding, annuals have particularly showy flowers. This is because they flower for only one season, so in the short time they're around they need to quickly attract pollinators and set seed to ensure their survival.

COSMOS 'PURITY'

If you're a seed-growing enthusiast, these are the plants for you. For colour throughout summer and often into autumn and winter, simply sow seeds either in pots or directly into the soil in late autumn, late winter or spring (depending on the species).

One of my favourites are **annual poppies** with their cheerful bright red flowers. **Opium poppies** (*Papaver somniferum*) are also a fantastic addition, with silver foliage and dark purple flowers. There are **sweet peas** (*Lathyrus odoratus*) with their heady scent and ability to climb over any structure in a single season. They also make great cut flowers. **Marigolds** (either **French *Calendula*** or ***African Tagetes***) are another favourite. Their intense colour and ability to survive anywhere as well as warding off nasty pests in the vegetable patch make them a must-have. **Nasturtiums** (*Tropaeolum majus*), also work well in your vegetable garden as companion plants; they are stunning, spread quickly and every part is edible. They are a fantastic option for the seed growers.

Sunflowers (*Helianthus annuus*) are great to grow with children because they are very easy to grow and make a big impact in one year, with soaring heights, massive flowers and seeds for both human and animal consumption. ***Pelargoniums*** (often incorrectly called geraniums) can be grown in the garden or in patio or balcony containers. They are not technically annuals, as they will grow year after year where temperatures never fall below freezing, but in temperate climates they are treated as annuals, dispensed with at the end of the growing season, or brought indoors for the winter.

Morning glories (*Ipomoea*) are grown as annuals in temperate regions, too, and I think they are very beautiful (despite being closely related to bindweed) as they grow in a similar way, occupying an enormous space but producing prolific colourful, trumpet-shaped blooms followed by attractive seeds. There are headily scented **stocks** (*Matthiola*) and tender **salvias** (ornamental sages) that also bring zing to the garden with a range of different foliage and flower colour, often scented foliage adding another dimension of interest. **Cosmos** is an old favourite, with bright, daisy-like flowers and delicate foliage. If you are looking for maximum impact, try ***zinnias***, ***rudbeckias*** and ***dahlias***. All are showy and striking and can look modern if planted carefully, either en masse or using a limited colour palette. Remove dahlia tubers from the garden in winter, store them in a cool, dry place and pot them up in spring – they will keep coming back year after year.

SUNFLOWER

MARIGOLD

RUDBECKIA

NICOTIANA SYLVESTRIS

NASTURTIUM

DAHLIA

BIENNIALS

Because biennials have a year of growth before they produce any flowers, many have the advantage of blooming relatively early in their second year, in late spring or early summer. As well as producing showy flowers, they often have impressive foliage, too.

Foxgloves (*Digitalis*), **giant Scotch thistles** (*Onopordum acanthium*), ***verbascums*** and ***echiums*** are just a few such species that make a big impact with their leaves and their flowers. Each throws up massive stalks or spires in their second year that bear towering flowers of bright yellow (*Verbascum*), blue (*Echiums*) or purple (*Onopordum* and *Digitalis*). Foxgloves will also come in a vast range of other colours with new cultivars being brought out regularly. And I find that many biennials (often more so than annuals) will release their seed around their base once they've finished flowering and seedlings will spring up in abundance the following year. So although these plants only seemingly give for two years, their offspring can go on to grace your garden for years to come.

VERBASCUM

PLANTS FOR SHADE

SKIMMIA JAPONICA This is a great shrub for a shady position – it will even cope where the shade is very dry.

BRUNNERA MACROPHYLLA 'JACK FROST' this perennial forget-me-not adds colour both in terms of its beautiful variegated foliage and also its tiny blue flowers. This is a valuable ally in difficult shade.

HOSTA SPP. Apart from being famously guzzled by slugs and snails, hostas will thrive in the shade, where other plants have great difficulty. They do need some moisture but provided they get that they should do absolutely fine.

VINCA MAJOR/MINOR Periwinkle is a brilliant scrambling plant for shady positions. It will send out runners here, there and everywhere and really spread with vibrant blue flowers and evergreen, often variegated foliage, meaning that it really earns its keep.

HEDERA SPP. Ivy is a great choice for shade. If you choose carefully and pick a delicate, variegated cultivar that will climb, you can even create height by training these plants up the trees or walls.

MAHONIA SPP 'CHARITY' This shrub and many of its relations will thrive in the shade. It has very spiky leaves rather like over-sized holly leaves and yellow flowers early in the season that are often scented.

RUSCUS ACULEATUS Butcher's broom is a spiky character with thick, dark, small leaves. But where nothing else will grow this small shrub will thrive.

RUSCUS ACULEATUS

VINCA MINOR VARIEGATA

HOSTA SPP.

BRUNNERA MACROPHYLLA

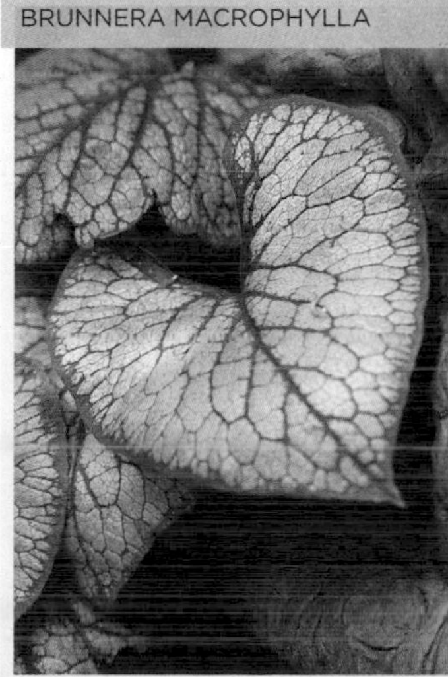

BULBS

There is something magical about planting bulbs in autumn that stay well below the surface of the soil all winter – just long enough for you to forget that you planted them. Then, in the earliest stages of spring, a little shoot will break through the soil and within a matter of weeks you have a beautiful flower that will come back year after year.

ALLIUM SEED HEAD

Although usually associated with spring, there are bulbs for every season of the year – from the earliest snowdrops, crocuses and reticulated iris in winter and early spring, through to tulips and daffodils a little later, camassias and alliums in late spring and early summer and *Colchicums* rearing their pastel-coloured heads in the autumn. There is a huge range available, from all around the world, and with such a wide choice you should certainly find suitable bulbs for your site, soil and tastes.

Tulips are always stunning and there are hundreds of wonderful, colourful varieties. 'Appledorn' is the classic red cultivar and I find it hard to beat for impact. 'Queen of the Night' is a deep purple, almost black, which sits beautifully in amongst the softer colours traditionally associated with spring flowers. One of my favourites, though, is 'Spring Green' with green, turning to cream, flowers that are delicate and elegant. You may find you need to replace tulips every three or so years. You can lift your tulips once they have finished their display and try storing them for replanting the following autumn to get more from your bulbs.

Daffodils (*Narcissus*) are an old spring favourite and nowadays there is an immense range, with an abundance of new varieties. As well as bigger, bolder, brighter yellow ones some are white, scented, dwarf, multi-flowering (known as multi-headed). Try them and see which you like. The multi-head cultivars are increasingly popular with 'Tete-a-Tete' perhaps one of the most acclaimed. For a big, bright, classic flower try 'St Patrick's Day'. The peacock daffodils make an interesting change with their multi-coloured trumpets in the centre of their white flowers, which might be worth trying. For something really interesting try 'Mondragon'. This cultivar has a deep orange centre that looks more like additional petals.

Reticulated irises and beauty irises have to be a firm favourite, with colouration on the petals that looks like a tiger's stripes or a bee's stomach. They come in soft blues, whites and deep purples and the former gets no taller that 15cm (6in). Other smaller plants like scillas, chinodoxas and hyacinths will always liven up your outdoor space in early spring with colours ranging through blues and purples and in the case of the hyacinth, shades of pink and primrose, and a stunning scent. *Fritillaria* – particularly the snakehead group, is another stunning bulb. The reptilian markings on their hanging, rounded petals make them a must-have. Camassias stand tall but dainty and really evoke a cottage-garden feel in shades of white, pink and blue, reaching heights of up to 50cm (20in). And if you're looking for something really modern, you cannot go wrong with an allium. They tend to flower a little later than lots of other bulbs and are usually purple or white. Some have a sparkler-like effect created by the flower formation, while others are perfectly spherical. Most flowers stand on stalks of around 60cm (24in), but there are some varieties that produce huge flowers almost on the ground on a bed of strappy, long leaves.

PLANTING BULBS

Plant spring-flowering bulbs in autumn and autumn-flowering bulbs in spring. If you grow them in pots, then you can plant them out at any time of the year. Dig a hole with a trowel about three times the depth of the bulb. Place the bulb at the bottom of the hole with the roots facing down and the tip facing up. (If you can't tell which way is which then it doesn't really matter. A bulb will still grow upwards, it just has a longer distance to travel.) Cover the bulb with soil and firm down the soil gently. You don't usually have to water a bulb, especially in the autumn, but if it is exceptionally dry you may want to give the soil a light sprinkle.

GRASSES

Grasses have become the height of fashion in gardening. I would say they have taken the place of bamboo, but technically bamboo is a kind of grass, so maybe it would be more accurate to say that the trend for members of the grass family has moved on since the age of the mighty bamboo.

When choosing grasses, you'll find a vast range of colours, including numerous shades of green, white, yellow, bronze, red and purple; some have stripy leaves. They grow in tufts or clumps and range from being almost ground level to up to 2m (6.5ft) tall. Their flowerheads are often light and fluffy or feathery, adding to their tactile quality. One of the wonderful things about grasses is their ability to catch the light, giving them an elegance that is rarely achieved by other plants. They seem to glow as the sun shines through them, creating a mist-like effect in borders.

When it comes to maintenance, grasses are incredibly undemanding, which is another reason why they are so popular. Below are just some of the wonderful grasses available.

FEATHER REED GRASS

QUAKER GRASS (BRIZA MEDIA)

QUAKER GRASS
Briza media

As its common name suggests, the light, dainty flowerheads of this grass quake and shake in the slightest breeze. Other names include dithering-grass, jiggle-joggles, doddering-grass and totter-grass.

FEATHER REED GRASS
Calamagrostis x acutiflora 'Karl Foerster'

This is a rather large species reaching heights of 1.5m (5ft), but unlike the infamous pampas grass (*Cortaderia selloana*) feather reed grass has a transparent, fine quality that makes it much more versatile. If positioned at the back of a border, it gives height and can potentially obscure unattractive walls and fences; however, it will not obscure too much if planted at the front or in the middle of a border. Individual specimens can be placed among other plants to create sporadic features, or several can be grown en masse as a form of hedging. Its elegant flowerheads and striking architectural form provide interest for most of the year, but particularly in summer when it catches the evening sun.

BLUE FESCUE
Festuca glauca

This is a classic grass for a very exposed or coastal position. Forming a dense clump of

USING GRASSES IN THE GARDEN

Grasses are incredibly useful in the garden and serve many functions. The larger kinds make magnificent specimen plants, while some low-growing grasses provide excellent ground cover. In a mixed border, their vertical forms contrast beautifully with more rounded, broader-leaved plants, and they soften the planting scheme, so other plants work together more harmoniously. Grasses can also make a fantastic hedge – either low-growing grasses to edge a border or tall ones to demarcate a boundary or conceal areas of the garden. Many are evergreen, yet often change colour in autumn, so they provide a long season of interest. Very importantly, grasses bring movement into a space. The way they sway, rustle or whip in the wind creates different sensations – either of calm or excitement – and produces interesting sounds.

fine but very tough electric-blue foliage, it can be quite striking. Blue fescue will soften a planting scheme if grown among other plants, or create a dramatic effect if used in isolation or on the edges of a display.

MAIDEN GRASS
***Miscanthus sinensis* 'Morning Light'**

I bought this elegant grass for when I first started gardening; all these years later, it reliably comes up year after year, never gets too big for its allotted space, and softens the other plants around it. All *Miscanthus* grasses have distinctive, white-ribbed leaves; this particular cultivar has a fine, vertical stripe all the way up each leaf, which catches the light and produces a silvery effect. The flowerheads are red and fairly robust compared with other grasses.

PANICUM SPP.

This has millions of sprays in gentle explosions of wispy seeds. It is simply stunning when planted en masse.

MAIDEN GRASS (MISCANTHUS SINESIS)

There are two kinds of *Panicum*. The annual varieties are the more delicate with a mist-like explosion of seed above stems and leaves that are often purple. They need to be sown every year and planted out, though they might well seed themselves in addition. They are stunning.

The second form is the perennial *Panicum,* which is far more sturdy and has seed heads with a much more robust form. It can have the same purple hues but also comes in green. This is a low-maintenance option but you may not find it quite as enticing as its annual cousin.

PENNISETUM

PENNISETUM SPP.

This species is often annual, sometimes perennial but often tender, so will need overwintering in a cold frame or greenhouse. Otherwise known as millet, *Pennisetum* has one defining characteristic and that is the plume of delicate and fluffy seeds that appear on heads reminiscent of a kitten's tail.

They come in a variety of shades though the most dramatic are annual with deep purple foliage and flowerheads. The perennials are often purple and have a rather more delicate form than the annual cultivars.

STIPA TENUISSIMA

MEXICAN FEATHER GRASS
Stipa tenuissima

One of the most common grasses used in planting schemes, Mexican feathergrass is instantly appealing and adds dramatic impact to a border. Green at the base and soft yellow at the tips, the very fine, almost hair-like flowerheads give this grass an incredibly soft, almost silky appearance. It will grow in most conditions and needs minimal care. If you have very limited space, a good alternative is *Carex comans,* which comes in shades of gold, bronze and green. It is a timeless option that is a little smaller in size.

GRASSES FOR PARTICULAR SITUATIONS

Most grasses prefer full sun and moist but well-drained soil not too rich in nutrients. If you're susceptible to very cold snaps or heavy frosts, you will need something really tough. *Molinia* (purple moor grass) is one such species, and it also tolerates acidic soils and shade. If you have a damp area, choose *Deschampsia* (hair grass), as it will cope with fairly constantly moisture.

PLANTS FOR A SEASIDE GARDEN

I grew up by the sea and have friends that live right on the beach, so I know the pain of trying to create a successful garden in such conditions. The main problems you will face are from the salt and the wind. Salt will either hit your plants from above in stormy weather or permeate through the soil to attack plants from the root. Here, I have a few suggestions of flowers that will tolerate seaside conditions. Even if you're landlocked, you could consider using these plants in the garden, as they're attractive in their own right.

SEA KALE
(Crambe maritima) has curly leaves that are deep purple when they emerge in spring and then turn dark green. They are large leaves with a rubbery feel. Sea kale also produces sprays of white flowers with a beautiful scent, especially when planted en masse. These flowers then turn into pea-like edible seeds which have a salty taste. The leaves of sea kale can also be harvested, and if blanched and mixed with a little melted butter are delicious and very good for you.

SEA THRIFT
(Armeria maritima) is a classic seaside plant that you'll often find growing by the coast. It has small tufts of grass-like foliage above which are borne little pompoms of pink flowers on stalks about 10cm (4in) high. They are very dainty and pretty and, if all else fails, they are a guaranteed success in a coastal garden.

SEA BUCKTHORN
(Hippophae spp.) is a shrub that produces super food in the form of a bright orange fruit. The fruit is an acquired taste, with a sharp flavour but the shrub itself is a lovely looking plant with delicate, thin, silver leaves. It will grow happily by the sea but is particularly fond of a sandy soil. Be warned that this shrub can take over a space if left unchecked.

HEBES are a great shrub for a coastal position. They grow really well and become lush where other plants can suffer. With glossy, evergreen leaves and flower spikes ranging from deep purple through to white, they really earn their keep.

NEW ZEALAND FLAX
(Phormium tenax) is a great coastal choice. It will survive in even the most barren seaside position.

CABBAGE PALM
(Cordyline australis) is another similarly exotic plant that will thrive by the sea. Be warned not to mix the tropical and naturalistic looks as they do not work well together. If you are going for palm-like plants, stick with those and try to find similar tropical-looking companions with bold foliage. Mallow is a good option, or *agapanthus*, which will also survive if protected from the worst of the salt. Mixing delicate cottage garden plants with tropical counterparts will create a confusing and inharmonious design.

SEA HOLLY
(Eryngium spp.) is perhaps the most widely used in horticulture because it is strikingly beautiful with white or vibrant, electric-blue spiky flowers and glossy leaves, often heavily and psychedelically veined.

ANNUALS are great for the seaside. You will need to replace them every year, but where other things struggle to grow, plant out plugs of annual poppy, marigolds, corn flowers, linseed and many other annual crops that will provide much-needed colour.

BULBS AND CORMS are also a great colour injection for a coastal position. Plant them with a healthy dose of compost, or even manure in extreme areas, and they should really do well. You might want to protect your bulbs further by keeping them in containers and planting those when the bulbs flower, bringing them in through the stormy winters where the winds and waves will increase the salt levels. The range that will survive will surprise you. Tulips, daffodils, alliums and crocosmia should all be absolutely fine in a coastal position with some TLC.

POND PLANTS

If you have a pond, you will find that its appearance is dramatically improved by the presence of some planting. In fact, plants are essential to keep the water clean, unless you're using a pump or a filter. They also make the space really valuable for wildlife. There are four main types of plant that you need to include in your pond in order to ensure a healthy ecosystem, each performing a different function: deep-water aquatics, oxygenators and marginals. In some cases, a pond or waterway will create a damp or flood-prone region immediately next to the water. This will require either bog plants or flood-tolerant plants depending on the levels and regularity of moisture.

HORSETAIL (EQUISETUM ARVENSE)

WATER LILY (NYMPHAEA)

Deep-water aquatics

The most popular deep-water plants are the highly ornamental water lillies (*Nymphaea spp.*). They have showy flowers with a rubber-like texture in all different sizes and colours. These flowers, along with the generous round leaves, float on the water's surface while the roots sit on the base of the pond.

Choose your species carefully, as water lilies all have varying depth requirements. If your pond is too deep for the species you want, you can always sit the plant on bricks or rocks to bring it up to the correct level. The plants spread across the water's surface throughout the season and will come back each year without any trouble. Do not over-plant, otherwise you'll see only lily and no water. And also be aware that these are quite hungry plants.

Other deep-water plant options include the water hawthorn (*Aponogeton distachyos*), which is very pretty with delicate, white flowers, and the brandy bottle (*Nuphar lutea*), which resembles a water lily in some ways but produces small yellow flowers that look rather like those of a buttercup.

Oxygenators

Oxygenating plants improve the quality of the water. Even though they're not the most attractive of plants, you do need to include them in your pond otherwise the water will become cloudy, full of algae and generally unpleasant, and your other plants might struggle to survive.

The best oxygenators are ones that aren't going to take over, as many have a tendency to do. Ideally, choose native plants, as some non-natives can get a bit out of control. Hornwort (*Ceratophyllum demersum*) and spiked water milfoil (*Myriophyllum spicatum*) are two effective species for use in British ponds, and water violet (*Hottonia palustris*) oxygenates while also looking pretty. It has tiny leaves and pink flowers that stick up above the water's surface.

The more plants you get to fill your pond, and particularly block the light, the more you will reduce the risk of algal growth in the water and the more protection you will provide for visiting wildlife. I also think a pond full of plants happens to look much more attractive.

Marginals

Marginal plants sit in the shallow water at the edge of the pond, as they do not like to be submerged too deeply. You have the most options with marginals, as there are numerous species that need these conditions. Marginal plants soften the pond's edges and help it blend in with its surroundings.

Barred horsetail (*Equisetum japonicum*) is a striking plant with bold spears that stick up from the water. The plants can be softened with more gentle foliage surrounding them, or they can be used in isolation for dramatic impact in a more modern planting scheme.

The American blue flag iris (*Iris versicolor*), the long-time favourite among gardeners, has a beautiful blue or purple flower. If you want something brighter, the yellow flag (*Iris pseudacorus*) is a good choice. It grows taller than its versicolor cousins and has a reputation for spreading quickly, but if you have a pond large enough to accommodate it it's a beautiful addition.

The flowers of the water forget-me-not (*Myosotis scorpioides*) are similar in appearance to the forget-me-not, with pale blue flowers with white, pink or yellow centres borne in small clusters.

Watermint (*Mentha aquatica*) has fluffy, pale lilac flowers and green leaves that have a pink hue and are mint-scented. The foliage stays quite low, so it will not obscure the view of the water but will soften the edges of the pond. It is attractive and its fragrance is pleasing, but it can take over a pond, so if you have limited space, plant with caution.

The common or soft rush (*Juncus effusus*) is a very distinctive, native plant that grows as a marginal while giving gentle, architectural height. *Juncus* comes in many forms, including spiralled varieties and some that have leaves that look more like those of an iris.

BULRUSH

BOG PLANTS

Gunnera macrophylla
Macro means big and *phylla* means leaf. This plant does what it says (in Greek) on the tin. Each leaf on this plant can grow to well in excess of 1m (3ft). It has a dinosaur-skin-like texture to the leaf and stem surface and creates a wonderful Jurassic feel. Cover the crown of the plant in winter to protect it from the frost – people often use the cut-back leaves to do this. It is worth adding that it is not a good idea to plant this species next to a waterway as in some regions it can be classified as an invasive species.

Persicaria spp.
These delicate plants topped with little elongated lollipops of pink or white flowers thrive in a moist bog and need very little maintenance (see image right). They are also attractive and floral where many other bog plants are not.

Ligularia spp.
A few popular cultivars of this are available but 'The Rocket' is perhaps the most commonly used as it has such striking foliage and huge spires of orange flowers. It will certainly add flamboyance to your pond.

Filipendula spp.
This genus has heavily margined and attractive leaves with flowers, usually in white or pink, that plume like feathers from the plant's top. They offer a sophisticated option for the bog area around the pond.

Rodgersia spp.
This plant has the appearance of being very ancient. The palmate leaves are large and give the impression of prehistory and drama. They thrive where it is wet and will provide lush greenery for the boggy areas of the garden.

Astilbe spp.
This is such a popular plant that people often try to plant it in their gardens regardless of the moisture levels, without much success. It can cope with a little drought but will need regular drenching and thrives best in permanently moist conditions. It has tall plumes of purple, pink or white flowers and delicate foliage.

FLOOD-TOLERANT PLANTS

When planting plants that may be exposed to periodic flooding, choose specimens with a strong root system as this will help them to take as much water as possible up into the stems where small, weak root systems might well begin to rot.

Plants that cope with flooding are ones that have adapted to areas where they have to deal with periods of dry weather and periods of wet. This is the difference between flood plants and bog plants which have to cope with near constant wet or damp conditions. There are a lot of plants that can cope with both, however, and making use of such forgiving plants also saves you a lot of effort in aftercare.

SHRUBS
Guelder Rose (*Vibirnum opulus*)
Dogwood (*Cornus sanguinea/alba*)

HERBACEOUS (TALL)
Sneezeweed (*Helenium*)
Michaelmas daisy (*Aster*)
Culver's root (*Veronicastrum*)
Hemp agrimony (*Eupatorium cannabinum*)

HERBACEOUS (MEDIUM)
Siberian iris (*Iris sibirica*)
Plantain lilies (*Hosta*)
Montbretia 'Lucifer' (*Crocosmia* 'Lucifer')
Black-Eyed Susan (*Rudbeckia*)

HERBACEOUS (SMALL)
Periwinkle (*Vinca*)
Columbine (*Aquilegia*)
Elephant's ears (*Bergenia*)

GRASSES AND RUSHES
Soft rush (*Juncus effusus*)
Pendulus sedge (*Carex pendula*)
Zebra grass (*Miscanthus sinensis*)
Switchgrass (*Panicum virgatum*)

FERNS
Royal fern (*Osmunda regalis*)
Broad buckler fern (*Dryopteris dilatata*)

15
P
7
N
11
K
Potassium.
Bone meal
Beans

CHAPTER 6
FRUIT, VEGETABLES & HERBS

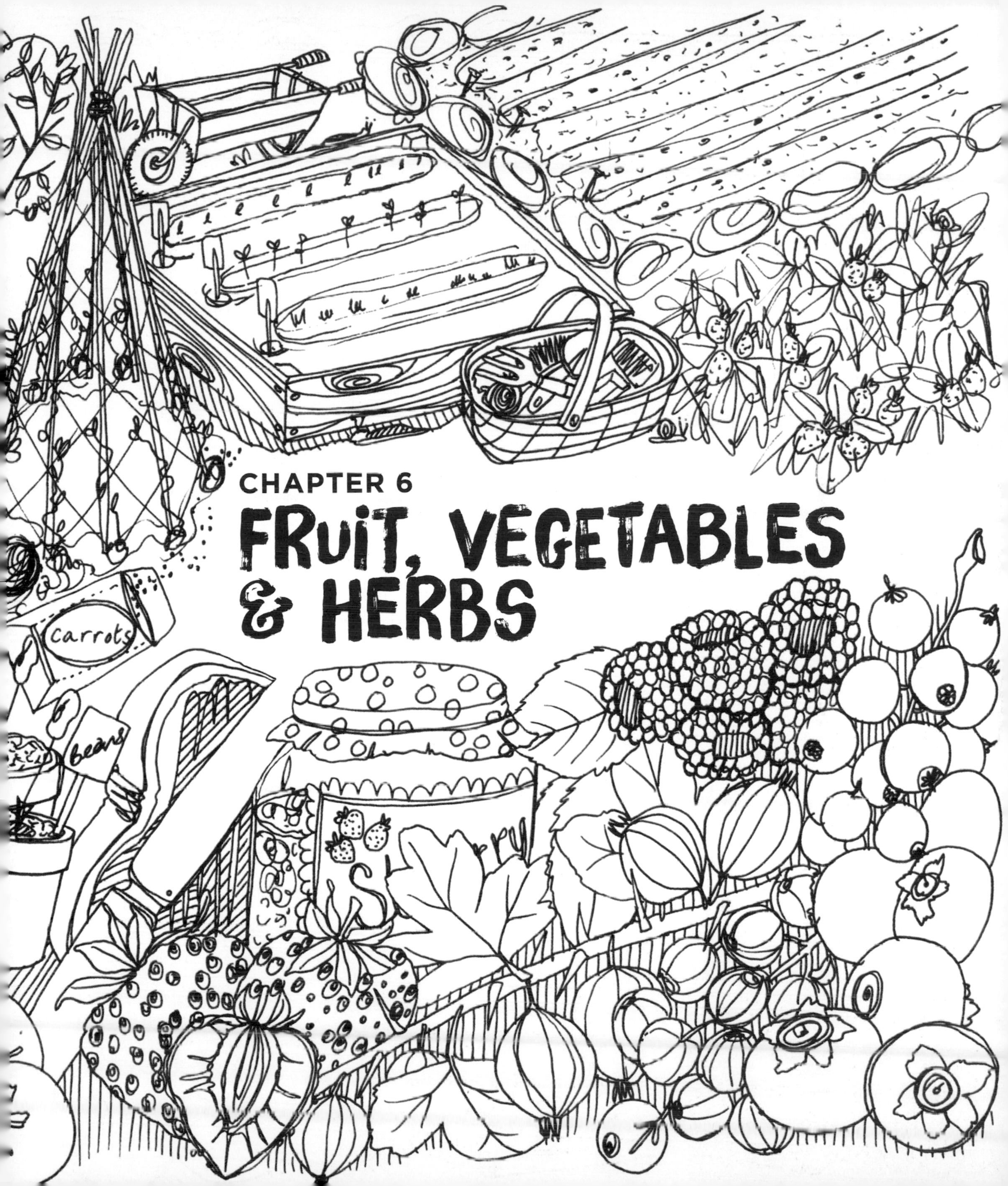

There is nothing as enjoyable as pottering around your garden, popping things into your mouth as you go. Although you can buy a great variety of fruit and vegetables in the shops all year round, they never taste as good as when they're home-grown, ripe and warmed from the sun, and plucked straight from the branch or stem.

ONIONS RIPENING

PURPLE CARROTS

Think about what produce you'd like to grow – this will probably be what you and your family like to eat. However, bear in mind that everything tastes better when it's home-grown and it pays to keep an open mind. Also, remember that some crops demand a lot more attention and space than others, so be realistic about how much time you can devote to their care and concentrate on growing those crops that are really worth cultivating in your garden.

To grow vegetables and fruit you need a sunny situation, ideally with a wall or fence nearby, to provide shelter, retain heat and, in some cases, reflect light. The soil needs to be deep, rich and well-drained. If it isn't up to scratch, there are ways you can improve it, such as digging in organic matter (see page 192). Alternatively, grow crops in raised beds or containers filled with multipurpose compost and place them in a sunny site.

It is true that in any garden the key is the soil the plants grow in, but with vegetable and fruit growing, a healthy soil becomes all the more important. To get it to a healthy state before you start, you can add all kinds of soil improvers and create deep beds of beautiful growing medium by digging down or building up and filling a large space with top-quality soil. You then have to keep your beds rich in nutrients to guarantee a high yield and high-quality crops. Regular watering, feeding, weeding and some form of mulch will keep your veg beds in peak condition during the growing season, and in between crops a large dose of manure or rich compost and ensuring you rotate your crops regularly (i.e. do not grow the same crop in the same bed year after year) will make your vegetables grow as well as they can.

The reason for rotating crops is fairly simple. Each plant uses nutrients in different quantities. Planting the same crop each season will mean that one area of land will be depleted of specific nutrients and others will be plentiful. Moving your crops around, specifically growing a different family of vegetables in a bed each year, prevents an imbalance of nutrients in the soil. Certain families of plants also replenish the nutrient supply, making them great to grow all over the garden and saving you money and time in buying and digging in manure. Legumes, for example, fix nitrogen in the soil.

Another important reason for rotating your crops is that certain crops are susceptible to specific diseases to which others are immune. Growing the same crop every year runs the risk of those diseases being able to really take hold in a bed. If you change the crop you can prevent a certain fungus or bacteria from becoming too strong, again preserving a more natural balance. There are some diseases that will stay in the soil for a long time, regardless of what is growing there. Club root, for example, is a disease that stunts the growth of members of the brassica family (that's cabbage, kale, sprouts and turnips, amongst other things) and it will stay in the soil for around twenty years. If you keep planting a brassica in that soil, that will add another twenty years onto the life of the disease. The answer is to plant non-brassicas or, preferably, to dig out and replace all the affected soil before growing anything else to prevent the disease from spreading.

Obviously you cannot guarantee a disease-free vegetable patch by rotating your crops, but you can make it more likely that your plants will be as healthy as possible.

Your vegetable patch is also a place where you can be at your most creative. I've knitted garden string to grow beans up, woven baskets to protect crops from rabbits and grown carrots in old welly boots. Indulge more than just your horticultural creative juices!

PROVIDING NUTRIENTS FOR CROPS

Crop plants are a lot more work intensive for the gardener than ornamental plants, so you can't expect to just leave them alone and reap the benefits year after year. The key thing you need to provide is nutrients. Although flowers and trees do benefit from nutrients, usually there are enough of them in the soil to keep them afloat. With fruit and vegetables, which are much hungrier, it is an entirely different story.

BEFORE YOU PLANT

When preparing the soil before planting, you should add nutrient-rich organic matter, such as well-rotted manure or compost (see page 192) and slow-release fertilisers. As their name suggests, the latter break down slowly in the soil (over weeks or sometimes months) so the growing plants can make use of them as needed. Other forms of fertiliser are wood fire ash and green manure.

SLOW-RELEASE FERTILISERS

Poultry manure, blood, fish and bone, bonemeal and seaweed are all organic slow-release fertilisers that you can buy in pellet, powder or granular form. Select the types that are appropriate to the crops you're growing, bearing in mind the proportions of the three main plant nutrients: nitrogen (N), for leaf and stem growth; phosphates (P), for root growth; and potassium (K), for flower and fruit development. Sprinkle them onto the soil and water them in, or put a little in the soil as you plant. Don't use more than the guidelines on the packets advise, and for best results mix them well with soil first. If in doubt, use less than you think as over-fertilising can cause as many problems as it solves. And besides, you can always go back and feed the border again if you didn't put enough feed down the first time.

GREEN MANURE

There are certain plants that will do wonders for your soil. Known as 'green manure', these are fast-growing crops (e.g. red clover, peas, beans and mustard) that are raised on empty beds (usually over winter) and then dug into the soil with their roots at least four weeks before planting your crops. They add nitrogen to the soil, increase the humus content, improve the soil structure and act as a weed suppressant.

WOOD FIRE ASH

Burning any wooden material that has not been Tanalised or treated with creosote produces an ash that is very rich in potassium. Sprinkle the ash onto the soil in winter, before planting or around the base of existing plants, and it will help the crops develop flowers and fruit.

FOODS FOR CROPPING PLANTS

Once the plants are growing, you need to give them a boost with liquid or soluble feeds. These get washed through the soil fairly speedily, but you will see a difference to the plant within a matter of minutes sometimes.

There are a number of options for feeds, both organic and chemical (inorganic). Although it's good to try to be organic where we can, there are some advantages to chemical fertilisers. They give you greater control about when and how the plant can benefit from their effects, they tend to be more balanced, and provided you follow the instructions you can avoid the problem of over-feeding.

Those that are available in liquid or soluble form include tomato feed (which can be used for any flowering or fruiting plant), seaweed extract and general-purpose feed.

HOME-MADE ORGANIC FEED

You can make your own organic liquid fertiliser from comfrey, which makes an excellent feed as it provides a good source of nitrogen and potassium. Pick the leaves, put them into a fine-mesh sack, which you immerse into water, and leave them to soak for a month or so, stirring occasionally in between. The 'tea' is ready when it turns dark brown, a little sludgy and starts to produce what can only be described as the most hideous smell known to man. Dilute it to look like weak tea and apply it with a watering can. Comfrey tea also helps to activate a compost heap, so pour a little bit of it on to the surface.

FRUIT

I've selected the top fruits that I think you should try in your garden, as they're tasty, productive and easy to grow. In some ways, fruit is easier to grow than vegetables, and they remain in their positions year after year, so you don't have to take crop rotation into account as you do with vegetables.

CHERRY
(Prunus spp.)

The cherry is wonderfully useful in the garden. It produces blossom in the spring that goes on to produce fruit. Make sure you buy a fruiting variety of cherry, though, as some are only ornamental and although they produce a lovely display of blossom, they are in fact barren. Fruits like cherry that have one single stone at their centre, are known as drupes.

It is worth looking at the many different varieties of cherry that are available to make sure you buy one that produces the kind of fruit you want. 'Montmorency' is one of the most popular tart cherries, with bright red fruit, which can be used in cakes and jams where sugar is added. If you have only a little space then 'North Star' is a recommended dwarf variety. For a sweet cherry that can be eaten straight from the tree try 'Glacier' or 'Compact Stella' for something more compact.

And while we are talking about the genus *Prunus*, look at plums, 'Victoria' being my personal favourite but others, such as 'Blue Tit', have a compact habit. Even apricots (*Prunus armeniaca*) make a great alternative. And if you have a mild climate, a warm and sunny south-facing wall or are lucky enough to have a glass house then why not try growing a peach tree (*Prunus persica*)? If you are growing it indoors you will need to hand-pollinate it to guarantee fruit but it will be well worth the effort. Peaches from the tree always taste better than they do from the supermarket. All of these trees will flower in spring, fruit in the summer to autumn and none will get too big for a small garden. In short, they will work hard for you and really earn their place in even the smallest space.

Do beware of fallen fruit and be vigilant in picking it up from the ground in order to avoid an invasion of wasps or ruining your lawn by mowing over fruit sludge.

APPLE

APPLE
(Malus spp.)

Apple is another great fruit tree as they will not get too big for a modest space and they provide a brilliant crop that can be used in cooking, eaten raw or preserved to be used throughout winter. I always like to think of aesthetics, even with growing fruit and veg, and apples can make a beautiful addition to any garden. They are often grafted onto a mature rootstock, which means they are ready to fruit as soon as you bring them home from the nursery and can also mean they are kept small if they are grown on a dwarf rootstock. Plants like this (called stepovers) make a fantastic small hedge or edge to a border. If you are really pushed for space then try to espalier your apples. Not only does it increase the yield but in my opinion it is a technique that looks absolutely stunning.

Grafting is fantastic, as once you have grasped the technique, which is rather involved and a little complicated but well worth the effort, you can attach different varieties of apple to the same tree, making the branches a riot of different colours – both the blossom and the fruits.

Apples are fully hardy and will grow in most soil types. They will not get to be much taller than 8m (26ft).

Apples come in a range of varieties that fruit from early summer ('Discovery' – a sweet red variety that doesn't keep very long but cannot be beaten if eaten from the tree) to varieties that fruit in the autumn like 'Cox's Orange Pippin', which is not only delicious from the tree but can also be preserved.

Then there are cookers like the famous 'Bramley' that are divine in puddings such as apple pie, apple crumble or simply baked with demerara sugar and water and served with cream.

Watch out for sawfly, codling moth, canker, brown rot and capsid bug. Most of these pests will affect the look of the fruit but codling moth often leads to a maggot found in the fruit and brown rot renders fruit inedible. Canker will eventually cause the tree to shed its branches.

PEAR
(Pyrus spp.)

A pear is another valuable asset to any fruit garden. They are closely related to apples and cherries and behave in a similar way. There are ornamental varieties that will not produce fruit but can add a lovely look. However, if it's fruit that you want, try 'Beth' for a high-quality, reliable crop with some disease resistance. If you are after taste then it is hard to beat the 'Conference' cultivar, which is so reliable that it often doesn't even need pollinating to produce fruits.

Both pears and apples will grow from seed but they will not grow true to form. That is to say they will not end up like the fruit they came from. They will grow to be a new variety. This may sound exciting but there is no guarantee that the variety will be remotely tasty or even produce an edible fruit, and what's more, it will often take up to 20 years before you get your first crop. In that sense it pays to buy a plant that has been grown by a nurseryman. However, if you are feeling adventurous and enterprising it doesn't hurt to experiment with sowing seeds of apples and pears.

BLUEBERRIES

The reason that I've included blueberries in my list of top fruits is that they're a fantastic fruit to grow if you have an acid soil; they even tolerate soils with a pH of less than 5. If you don't have an acid soil, you can grow them in pots of ericaceous compost. They are also one of the healthiest fruits you can eat. They are low in GI and high in anti-oxidants, so they're not fattening but will slow down the ageing process and improve your memory – apparently. Well, if there is even the slightest chance that any of the aforementioned facts are true, I'm willing to give them a try.

In terms of maintenance, these plants are very easy. They should be planted out in winter and do not need to be pruned for the first year or two, and then only once a year, in late winter. When pruning, remove a little of the old wood, as that will ensure that your bush is productive. With this regime you should get a good crop throughout the height of the summer and into early autumn.

The main thing when maintaining blueberries is keeping in mind that need for acidity. Water with rainwater rather than tap water if you can, and if your soil is tending to creep up the pH scale and become more alkaline, add iron filings or pine needles around the base occasionally. Avoid feeds used for other fruits, as they will be a little too rich for blueberries.

In terms of recommended varieties, 'Duke' is one of the hardiest and a good all-rounder. If you want something a little smaller but without compromising on the yield, try 'Top Hat'. It's a good choice for containers and small gardens.

CURRANTS

Although similar in many ways, blackcurrants, redcurrants and whitecurrants all differ in flavour. Blackcurrants are particularly delicious,

REDCURRANT

being juicy and mouthwateringly sharp. They are reliable but not as prolific as the red and white varieties. Redcurrants are very sharp, juicy and produce very reliable and plentiful crops. Whitecurrants are sweeter and less flavoursome than both their cousins, but they fruit well and reliably. Currants should generally ripen by midsummer.

You can grow currants as a freestanding bush, but I find they produce more fruit if grown as an espalier. This involves training the stems flat against a wall or fence so that they're horizontal or create a fan shape. Cut off any shoots that grow outwards from their support.

Pruning of espalier and bush red and white currants should take place in the autumn. Always remove any dead or diseased stems, keeping a nice open framework to allow air to pass through the plant, reducing the risk of future infections. You should not need to prune the plant for a year after planting, but in the autumn of its second season, and then annually from then on, remove around a third of the growth. Try to keep the shoots that have healthy, perpendicular growth and remove the ones that are inclined to grow towards the ground and the small stems that grow through the middle to discourage sawfly from laying eggs.

Blackcurrants are different and need to be pruned, in much the same way, but in the summer, straight after the fruits have finished. Container-grown currants will need repotting every two to three years.

Currants take up to two or even three years to start fruiting, so don't be downcast if you get nothing for a few years. If after some years they still haven't produced fruit, try feeding them a healthy mulch of manure in late winter or move them to a sunnier position.

GOOSEBERRIES

Gooseberries are such a versatile fruit, being ideal for jams, crumbles and lots of other puddings, as well as delicious straight from the bush. They can be white (green actually, but they are called 'white') or pink. The pink varieties tend to be a little sweeter in flavour, hence their name, dessert gooseberries. Choose your favourite, or grow one of each.

Gooseberries tend to do best as stand-alone shrubs either as standards (lollipop shaped) grafted onto a thick trunk, or at ground level. You may want to try tying them against a wall but I recommend that you wear a thick pair of gloves. There are a few thornless varieties but generally those with thorns will do serious damage!

New gooseberry plants need training to encourage a good, strong framework, and established ones need pruning to keep the crops coming thick and fast (see box, opposite). Also, put manure around the base in winter and apply a potassium-rich fertiliser throughout the growing season. Gooseberries can be propagated easily, either by layering or by taking cuttings in autumn (see page 196).

RASPBERRIES

Autumn-fruiting raspberries are easier to grow and take up considerably less space than the traditional summer-fruiting kinds, though watch out for suckers and thin the crops every few years or you might find your raspberry patch spreading into other

BEWARE OF THORNS!

Gooseberries have thorns, so harvesting the fruit can cause war wounds! The wood is very brittle, and thorns can snap off, so wear long sleeves or – even better – invest in a pair of long gloves, because sometimes little bits of plant material can get stuck in the skin and cause infections. Some varieties are called 'thornless', and although they're not truly thornless they are less thorny than the traditional kinds.

HOW TO PRUNE GOOSEBERRIES

NEW PLANTS

In the first year in spring, choose three or four evenly spaced stems that you want to produce the main framework of the plant and prune these back to about 20cm (8in) from the ground. Cut all the remaining stems right back to soil level.

ESTABLISHED PLANTS

In summer, after you've picked the fruit, cut all side branches that have grown in the current season back to about five buds. Leave the main branches as they are. The fruit will develop on the older wood, so pruning the newer growth from the tips does not affect your yield for the year. In winter, remove all dead, diseased and crossing shoots, as well as branches that touch the ground or are more than four or five years old. Shorten all the branch tips of your main stems by one quarter and cut side shoots back to three buds.

AUTUMN RASPBERRY

parts of the garden! They also produce fruit every year (unlike summer-fruiting ones, which are biennial), and are ready to pick from late summer to the first frosts. 'Autumn Bliss' is one of my favourite cultivars, with incredibly juicy, tasty fruits. They aren't fussy about soil, and come in yellow as well as red.

It's important to contain your raspberry plot. Grow the plants in a big pot or raised bed, or line the hole you plant them in with concrete slabs or thick plastic, otherwise they will spread. Unlike summer-fruiting raspberries, they don't need post-and-wire supports or tying in.

Give autumn-flowering raspberries a good feed in autumn and a little throughout the growing season, and prune them each winter, once they have stopped fruiting. Cut the stems right down to just above ground level and they will sprout new stems in spring.

STRAWBERRIES

There are numerous different varieties of strawberry, from the wild strawberry, which is only a few millimetres across, to 'Elsanta', which produces big, juicy fruits. You can get early, mid-season and late strawberries, so choose a variety that will be fruiting when you're around, otherwise the fruit will go uneaten! If you're a big fan, you could grow a selection of varieties that ripen at different times throughout the season, taste different and have fruits of varying sizes. Some varieties suit specific requirements, such as a shady situation or certain soil type.

Slugs adore strawberries, so grow them in hanging baskets or mounds surrounded by straw or copper rings, or scatter chilli powder generously around the plants. The straw also acts as a bed for fruits to rest on while they ripen, so they don't rot by sitting directly on the soil.

Cut back the foliage in autumn and remove the 'baby plants' that are produced on runners around the main plant or you may find yourself overrun! Every three or so years, however, keep those baby plants at the end of the runners as the parent plants will need to be replaced because as they get older they begin to produce less fruit. In terms of maintenance there isn't that much to remember. Give them a hard cut back, removing as much of the foliage as you can, in the autumn to get the last of the season's sunlight to the crown of the plant. It is also worth giving them a feed towards the end of the winter once they have finished setting their flower buds to give those flowers, which will turn into fruit, a real kick-start in the spring.

STRAWBERRY

VEGETABLES

The traditional way to grow vegetables is in straight lines, with wide soil paths between rows so you can walk through your crops to harvest, weed and feed plants easily. However, there is a move nowadays to make edible produce more visually interesting by incorporating the crops into your flower borders.

TURNIP

Although it is slightly trickier to reach the plants this way, some gardeners argue that growing your fruit and vegetables in among ornamental plants keeps weeds and pests at bay, as you will not be creating a monoculture. Problems can develop when you grow one type of crop on its own, because if a weed or pest or disease takes hold, it can spread quickly around the whole area and devastate the entire crop. Weeds out-compete plants that are more delicate, so planting something perennial or large (within reason) amongst a fragile crop can interrupt the spread of a weed.

A really good way of growing vegetables amongst other plants is to introduce some companion planting. The idea of companion planting is that by growing different plants together you maximise the potential for pollination and therefore yield and simultaneously protect the crop from pests and diseases. Certain plants, such as marigolds and nasturtiums, are used in a vegetable patch as sacrificial plants – creatures like slugs and aphids will target them in preference to the more important crops. Some really good combinations are tomatoes and cabbage or cucumber and nasturtiums.

Opposite are a few recommendations that I have for the novice vegetable grower to get you started.

RING THE CHANGES

Many vegetables have specific pests that attack them, so it's always good practice to mix it up a bit and plant slightly different crops each year so that no one pest has the chance to take hold too strongly.

BORLOTTI BEANS

CLIMBING FRENCH AND RUNNER BEANS

I would grow a crop of beans each year as part of your rotation. They're a pleasure to grow and taste delicious. They don't take up much room and their flowers are ornamental, so they're good for gardens where space is at a premium.

Sow the seed in a pot containing seed compost covered by a few centimetres of the same compost and keep it watered until the seedling pokes its first shoot above the soil. Once it's growing and all risk of frost is over, plant it into the garden next to a cane. As the plant grows it will wind its way around the cane. You can grow them in rows and set up lines of string or netting for them to climb up, or provide a structure such as a trellis.

If you water regularly, you'll find the cheerful red flowers give way to plump pods full of peas and pulses. They vary slightly in colour and shape, depending on which variety you choose, but all are delicious. I just love wandering among my rows of beans on a hazy summer afternoon, picking and eating them, still warm from the sun.

At the end of the year, either pull out the plants or cut them off at ground level. Like all legumes, the roots will have fed your soil with nitrogen, ready to benefit the next crop to be planted there.

CARROT HARVEST

CARROTS

Make sure you prepare your soil really well before sowing carrots, because if it's too stony the carrots will end up deformed. Sow seed directly into the soil throughout the spring about 3cm (1.25in) deep and about 5cm (2in) apart. When you can see the carrots growing, you may want to thin out the seedlings if any are too close together – this gives them room to grow. Ideally, try to sow them at this thickness from the start to avoid waste, as carrots rarely survive being transplanted. Avoid planting carrots into soil that has been very recently manured as this extra nutrient can cause them to fork – which is when the roots divide and the carrots, although they still taste alright, will not have the juicy, single tap root.

To grow good edible roots, you need soil high in phosphate, so when feeding carrots look for an option with high phosphorous content. For an organic choice, use bat manure or bonemeal. If you are using a chemical feed then look at the second letter of the nutrient content ratios (P). Harvest your carrots in the summer of their first year; if the plants are left to the second year, they will bolt.

Harvesting is best done in the evening to avoid trouble with carrot fly. These small flies lay their eggs on the soil and the larvae then burrow down to attack the root. Luckily the carrot fly only flies near the ground so a physical barrier of about 60cm (24in) in height will be sufficient to keep the flies off your crops. Something like polythene will be perfect for this. It's also another good reason for planting carrots in the correct spacing, as the smell of carrot seedlings being pulled up attracts female carrot flies. Sowing carrots later in the spring when the first brood is over will prevent infestation. Sowing in succession throughout the spring will mean that you can harvest carrots throughout the summer. And the really good news is that they need hardly any water at all. In terms of maintenance they could not be easier.

RHUBARB

This is a great vegetable. It is so versatile, being useful in both savoury and sweet dishes, though it is usually used more like a fruit than a vegetable. It's also incredibly easy to grow. The main problem you'll have is controlling its spread and it may need thinning or dividing every few years.

For really tender stems, generally harvested in the very early spring, you can 'force' rhubarb to make the stems grow fine and pale. Cover the crown of the plant with a rhubarb forcing pot or an upturned flowerpot in winter. If you want additional heat, you can also add some straw to increase the temperature, though this is not strictly necessary, and it is important not to pack it in too tightly as this can restrict the growth of those stems. Once the stems have grown to the top of the pot, uncover and leave the plant to grow a little longer, then harvest it in spring. This crop will come back year after year and might need dividing or thinning every few years. Do not eat the leaves as they are poisonous.

RHUBARB

RUBY CHARD

A good mulch in the winter will protect the crowns of the rhubarb from the worst frosts and also give a feed in readiness for the following season's growth.

SWISS CHARD

Very similar to perpetual spinach, except this comes in fantastical colours and has slightly thicker midribs. Ruby chard is a brilliant crimson with green leaves, and it also comes in rich yellow- and green-stemmed varieties. Swiss chard can be harvested throughout the year; take what you need to eat and the leaves will grow back. It's easy to grow, tasty and healthy, and can be eaten raw in a salad or cooked.

The main problem with growing chard or perpetual spinach is bolting. This is when a vegetable flowers, making it less tasty and less succulent. More often than not, when a plant bolts it needs to be dug up and disposed of. It will be more likely to bolt as the weather gets hotter and, particularly, if the roots get too hot. There are a few ways you can avoid bolting (see page 179).

Be aware that it is not always a bad thing if a vegetable flowers. Beans and peas need to flower in order to produce their crop. Tomatoes (though of course technically they are fruits) are the same.

TOMATOES

Although tomatoes are technically fruits, no vegetable patch is complete without them. Their deep red fruits are incredibly evocative of high summer, and their heavily scented foliage is one of my favourite smells. (The leaves are poisonous, so don't try to eat them!)

Tomatoes come in a huge range of different shapes, sizes and flavours, so there are plenty of different varieties to try. 'Gardener's Delight' is a very popular variety of tomato, recommended for both its yield and its flavour. This is a type of cherry tomato, which is very commonly grown. Beef varieties such as 'Better Boy'

TOMATO

and 'Carmello' are noted for their flavour and the former is even fairly disease resistant. Plum tomatoes such as 'San Marzano' are the best tomatoes to use for cooking and this particular variety is famed for its intense flavour once cooked. Be aware that the larger the fruit, the more support you will need to give your plants. The stems of tomatoes are fairly fleshy and you must tie them up either on canes, strings or other structures to avoid the plant breaking any of its limbs. You will need to do this for most tomatoes although some small bush varieties are self-supporting but cordons (plants that produce fruit on one long stem) and large fruits will always need to be given support. You can grow them in the garden or greenhouse, and they do well in containers or in grow bags, which act as pots and compost all in one.

As annuals, tomatoes can be grown from seed or bought as small plants each year. Sow seeds in a seed compost in cells, laying them on the surface and covering with a fine layer of sifted seed compost. Water the seeds then cover with a plastic bag to give them a humid and warm environment. As soon as the seeds have germinated and the first leaves are beginning to grow, remove the bag (if left on at this stage it can lead to 'damping off', which is a fungus that can kill the plants). Once your seedlings are strong, pot them on into a bigger container for the season. Although tomatoes can grow outside, make sure you gradually acclimatise them by taking them out in the mornings and bringing them back in at night for a few weeks before leaving them out for good.

Once growth of the plants is well under way, 'pinch out' (remove with your fingertips) every third or fourth side shoot to get the best yield from your tomatoes. Also, thin the foliage once the fruits start to develop so the tomatoes have full exposure to maximum sunlight so they can ripen.

Tomatoes require a high potassium feed (you can buy tomato food at any garden centre). Feeding should be done after the first truss of flowers is turning to fruit and repeated roughly every two weeks.

Tomatoes are very susceptible to a disease called blight. Potatoes, which are in the same family, also suffer from this. Unfortunately, blight is a fungal disease, carried on the air by spores over great distances. If you are in an area that suffers from blight and you attempt and fail to grow tomatoes there are a few things that you can do. Try growing them in a greenhouse, which reduces the risk of the spores hitting your crop. If you think the problem is in your soil, then try growing tomatoes in containers and buying in topsoil or compost. You must then replace this compost each year. Keep your tomatoes well ventilated as blight thrives in humid, warm and damp areas. Finally, if none of these methods work, only buy varieties that are specifically labelled as 'blight resistant', such as 'Better Boy'.

Another problem that often occurs in tomatoes is blossom end rot. This disease turns the bottom of the tomato black. This is basically caused by a deficiency in calcium so make sure you give your plants a good, regular feed to keep nutrient levels high.

TO HELP THE RIPENING PROCESS

If it's getting towards the end of the season and your tomatoes have still not ripened, pick the fruit, put them on a sunny windowsill indoors and put a ripe banana with them. Bananas secrete ethylene, which is a natural plant hormone in the form of a gas, which is responsible for fruit ripening. If exposed to this your tomatoes still have a chance to ripen.

CAVOLO NERO

KALE AND CABBAGE

These are members of the brassica family, which are long lived, healthy and grow throughout the season. You can buy small plants or grow them from seed and apart from thinning, regular harvesting and pinching out to avoid bolting they require very little maintenance.

Members of the brassica family are susceptible to a disease called club root, which severely inhibits growth of the roots and will result in an extremely poor yield. The spores stay present in the soil for a long time so be sure to remove any affected soil and preferably avoid growing brassica in that spot for a good few years after the infection.

There are two other banes of the brassica grower's life. These are slugs and another little pest called cabbage white caterpillars. The slugs can be dealt with using the usual methods of barriers, beer traps and deterrents such as eggshells, hair or wool, chilli powder or salt. The caterpillars take a little more dealing with and they will munch through a cabbage leaf in no time at all. They are the larvae of the cabbage white butterfly and the best way to keep them at bay is by netting the plants, leaving a generous gap between leaf and butterfly to stop the female laying her eggs on the foliage. Otherwise you will need to regularly inspect and remove any eggs or caterpillars.

CUCUMBERS

Cucumbers can be grown indoors or outside. As they can take over a windowsill, more often than not they will be grown outside, unless you are lucky enough to have a greenhouse or polytunnel. For the best cucumbers, sow the seeds directly in the soil once all risk of frost has passed and then cover with a cloche (this can be the cut-off base of a plastic bottle to save money) or horticultural fleece. Feed the ground well throughout the growing season and make sure the soil is constantly moist. A sunny, moist and very fertile soil is best for cucumbers. Pinch out the growing tip of each non-flowering stem once they have seven leaves them. Leave all the flowers on once they appear. Cucumber plants can either trail along the ground or be tied to vertical strings. If you are growing them in a heated greenhouse, you can start this process in spring rather than early summer and if you do both then you will have cucumbers from summer to autumn.

Cucumber plants are fairly high maintenance and do suffer from a few ailments. Firstly, slugs and snails adore them, so be sure to protect them; chilli powder on the soil is the best method. Secondly, cucumber plants suffer from mildew, so when you are watering make sure you get as little water on the foliage as you possibly can. That way the fungus cannot get into the leaves.

PUMPKINS AND SQUASHES

Not for the faint-hearted or those with a modestly sized plot. The foliage is large, the plant is large and the fruit is large!

PUMPKIN

They are also some of the latest fruiting vegetables you can grow (unless you grow the thinner-skinned, early fruiting squashes), which makes them a really valuable addition in terms of aesthetics in the autumn and the winter. The fruits of pumpkins are generally orange and round whereas squashes vary greatly, often a similar orange colour but also commonly green, yellow, golden, grey or blueish and even very ornate combinations of different colours. The shapes are similarly varied and can verge on the weird and wonderful. This makes them a fantastic vegetable to grow with children, who love seeing the rapid growth and impressive fruits. Try the classic pumpkin, butternut squash, delicate squash, Rouge Vif D'Etampes pumpkins (beautiful and red), turban squash, table queen and white pumpkins.

To plant pumpkins and squashes (and you can grow them together), simply sow the seeds in spring directly into the soil and leave at least 1m (3ft) (preferably 2m/6ft) between each seed. Keep the plants well watered and fed and once they start producing fruit – especially if that fruit becomes very large – turn it periodically so that it grows into a nice, even shape, otherwise they tend to become flat on one side. Harvest from late summer, right through the autumn and store them in a cool, dry place for months after harvesting.

SWEETCORN

Sweetcorn is a wonderful crop and I like the delicate screening it provides. It can make a really interesting design feature and turn a space into something special.

Don't be fooled into thinking these are merely aesthetic additions, though. Sweetcorn is delicious and it comes in all kinds of colours (white, blue and gold) and sizes. The main thing you have to remember when you plant sweetcorn is that, unlike most garden vegetables, it needs to be planted in blocks rather than rows. This is because sweetcorn is wind pollinated so the more you have together the more likely you are to have successful fruit. If you grow them in a single row, it would take a very specific wind direction to pollinate them. So a nice block or square is the best method. There is one exception to this and that is if you intend to harvest them as mini sweetcorn, then you can harvest before fertilisation so the positioning does not matter.

Sow the seeds into the ground in spring and cover with plastic for better germination rates. Put them in a sunny position, which is sheltered from strong

winds otherwise they can collapse when they get tall. If the only space available is a little windy then you may need to stake the plants once they grow. Harvest the cobs once the tassels at the top have turned brown and the individual grains ooze a creamy liquid when squeezed.

LETTUCE

Lettuce is a great vegetable because with a regular sowing of seeds into cells of seed and cutting compost, you can create a succession of lettuce that will last throughout the summer. Plant out the seedlings once they have a few sets of leaves and water them well. You will need to keep them watered whilst they grow so ideally the beds should be constantly moist though not too wet.

There are many varieties of lettuce, which are divided into those with a loose formation of leaves, those that are more densely packed, forming a solid heart, and the ones in between. The classic 'Iceberg' or 'Little Gem' (a small lettuce) are heart-forming varieties; non-heart forming varieties are equally tasty but just have fewer leaves. A popular example is 'Lollo Rosso' which has curly, red leaves.

Do protect your lettuces from slugs by putting some sort of barrier such as wool, hair, eggshells, chilli powder or copper around the plants to keep these pests away.

ARTICHOKE

There are two kinds of artichoke. One is the Jerusalem artichoke, which is a species of perennial sunflower with edible tubers below the ground. They have lovely, cheerful, yellow flowers and an interesting flavour. Do be warned, though, because once you plant it, it is difficult to get rid of. Often even digging it out does not completely remove it and it may grow back the following year.

The artichoke that is perhaps more well known is the globe artichoke. This is a wonderful addition to the vegetable garden because it is delicious, comes back year after year and is stunningly beautiful. It looks like a thistle with a rosette of long, deeply toothed, silver leaves and tall, purple flowers on top of a perfectly round sphere of edible bracts. It is this that gives the vegetable its name and it is that part that you eat. Artichoke hearts are delicious and can be used to add a saline, olive-like but floral flavour.

GLOBE ARTICHOKE

They grow in a free-draining soil but need some nutrients to produce flowers. In terms of maintenance, they are very easy, requiring only a cut back each winter.

ASPARAGUS

This is a fantastic perennial vegetable. It grows in spring and if harvested will be cut as small spears. If left unpruned, though, they become a delicate, almost feathery plant that can develop plump, round, red berries at the end of summer.

Asparagus is quite an expensive vegetable to buy as you usually buy a bare-root plant rather than sowing seeds. The key with asparagus is to buy a few plants and let them spread, that way you save money. Another important thing to remember is that you need to give asparagus at least two years to mature before you start harvesting it.

Plant it in the autumn in deep beds, rich in nutrients and then leave them for two years. Early the following spring, you can start harvesting them by chopping them once they get to 15–25cm (6–10in) long. Give them a good feed every autumn.

If you have concerns about them taking up a large space for only a short season of interest, then you might want to think about growing them as a hedge or even in existing hedgerows, as asparagus will do well in either situation and add a really interesting feature to your boundaries.

HOW TO PREVENT BOLTING

Bolting can occur with various vegetables, including Swiss chard, perpetual spinach, lettuces, cabbages, garlic, onions and leeks. To prevent this from happening, follow the instructions below.

- **Mulch the soil around your plants to keep the roots cool.**
- **Start plants early. Prepare, buy or sow your plants in late winter or early spring so they don't get 'shocked' into flowering in the heat of summer. At worst, if they do bolt in the summer you will have enjoyed a spring's worth of harvest.**
- **Harvest little and often, which will act in the same way as pinching out tips and mean that the plant is constantly having to produce new shoots and not flowering stems.**
- **Pinch out growing tips regularly, so a flower spike can't form.**
- **Do not over-fertilise – particularly with potassium, as this will encourage flowering.**
- **Planting low-growing plants around the base of your vegetables can shade the roots and the soil.**

HERBS

Herbs, the fragrant plants used for seasoning dishes, enhance the garden in so many ways and are remarkably easy to grow. You don't need to have a dedicated herb garden – the lovely thing about herbs is that they're very ornamental and can mix seamlessly with other plants in pretty much any kind of border, their aromatic leaves providing long-lasting interest once neighbouring flowers have passed their prime. With many green, purple, gold and silver-leaved herbs, as well as the many variegated types, there is a huge choice available. Most herbs are perennial, so they will come back year after year.

THYME AND LAVENDER

The majority of herbs grow best in a sunny position in a light, free-draining soil, although there are some exceptions. Ideally, try to position your herbs near the house, so when you're cooking you can just pop out quickly and grab a little something or other to spice up your creations. Herbs grow very happily in containers, so you can always plant up a few of your favourites and place them conveniently near the back door, on the patio or balcony, or on the windowsill. If you have a reasonably heavy soil but would like to grow herbs in the garden, add plenty of gravel and sand to your herb beds before planting. If they don't thrive, you're probably better off growing them in containers filled with light, gritty compost.

Below are a few recommendations that I think would be a good starting point for any new herb-grower. However, this list does not even scratch the surface of what is available. There are old familiars like sage, parsley, coriander, dill, fennel, oregano, marjoram and basil, then there are the more daring or experimental ones like culinary lavender, curry plant, chervil, lovage, angelica, sweet cicely, nasturtiums (every part of which can be eaten) and so many more that I couldn't possibly list them all. Try things out, be bold, and enhance your garden with these plants as well as your kitchen.

BAY LAUREL

BAY

The bay tree is incredibly versatile in terms of design. It can eventually grow into a large evergreen tree, up to 6m (20ft) high, but it is often grown as a small bush or planted in large pots. One of its great benefits is it can be pruned into attractive round shapes – think of those lovely little lollipop bays. The fact that it can be pruned also means it makes a good hedge.

Bay has an amazing scent, too. The leaves are not directly edible, but the flavour they exude when cooked in a stew, soup or casserole is delicious.

Bay will grow well in most soil types as long as they are fairly free-draining. In temperate climates bay does not need protection from frost and it can survive in temperatures well below freezing, so as such it is classified as fully hardy.

BERGAMOT

BERGAMOT

A member of the mint family, this herb gives off a beautiful delicate aroma and the foliage is bolder than that of a lot of herbs, while retaining a dainty quality. The leaves are shaped like a jester's shoe – wide at the base, becoming pointed at the tip. This image is ratified by slight strokes of red that can occur along the leaf margins and veins. The leaves can be used to make tea; if added to a cup they can reproduce the flavour and aroma of Earl Grey.

This plant has some of the most striking flowers of all herbs. There are purple and red varieties borne at the top of each stem in crazy, punk-like florets.

Unlike most herbs, bergamot does not need full sun or a dry, free-draining soil. So any gardeners with clay soil or shadier conditions, take note! They actually need a fair bit of moisture to survive successfully.

Bergamot can suffer from mildew. This will not generally kill it off, but by the end of summer the foliage might have a white powdery substance on it and the whole plant looks unwell. Try cutting off the mildew as soon as you see it or try some mildew-resistant forms of the plants.

ENJOY THE FRAGRANCE

When deciding on herbs to grow, I suggest you go to the garden centre, have a good look at all the varieties on offer and – most importantly – smell them. Give the foliage a good rub between your fingers and then sniff. There are a few herbs that give off their scent most of the time, but generally movement stimulates the scents, so they're great for placing along the sides of a path, by garden gates or back and front doors. Drops of rain and light winds can also cause these plants to release their scents as leaves rub against each other, so it's worth taking a stroll down the garden, even in inclement weather!

CHIVES

Unlike the other herbs listed here, chives are not what I would describe as aromatic. However, they are incredibly useful – both in cooking and raw in salads. They are a member of the onion family and can be used as a milder substitute for onions or garlic, where the flavour of either of these might overpower other flavours.

Chives have totally upright, hollow stems and form little clumps that in one season will gain no more than 25cm (10in) in height – usually less. They will come back year after year and produce stunning, deep purple flowers. *Allium* 'Purple Sensations' is a very highly sought-after ornamental plant with striking flowers, and chives produce an extremely similar effect only in miniature. They look particularly spectacular when they catch the wind and their tufts of long-stemmed flowers create a gently swaying purple haze.

MINT

Mint has to be included on any list of herbs merely for staying power, but also, in many respects, for versatility. If you have tried, and failed, to grow herbs you will almost certainly have success with this fellow. Mint is mighty, and not just in the punch it can pack in the most robust of mouthwashes, but in its ability to survive and proliferate in any condition or aspect. And with multiple variants, you are sure to find one you like. There is apple mint, pineapple mint, chocolate mint, water mint and many more – all have a strong taste and smell of these other flavours along with the classic minty undertones.

If you don't want your garden to be swamped by mint, grow it in a container (you can sink this into the soil if you like). If you're brave enough to risk it in a border, avoid putting it near any small or fragile plants, or it will inevitably take over. But its heady fragrance and fresh flavour make growing it really worthwhile.

Mint will grow in most soil types but can cope with a little more moisture than classic Mediterranean herbs. If you are growing mint in a container, it will need feeding throughout the growing season and a mulch in winter. Every few years you can reinvigorate the plant by repotting it into a larger container or replacing the compost if it is not root bound.

ROSEMARY

I think planting this fantastic herb by any entranceway or path is an excellent idea. The aroma that oozes from the shrub will be released every time you brush past it.

Rosemary can grow up to 1.5m (5ft), but more commonly it's seen at around 50–100cm (20–39in). The traditional upright type gives evergreen structure to your borders, but there are also low-lying forms that can cascade over your walls or the edges of pots. It can be pruned back fairly vigorously to create a small hedge or rough topiary, but avoid going too far into the old wood or it may not re-shoot.

This fine plant produces tiny, delicate, electric-blue flowers that are gorgeous against the deep, dark green of the foliage. It has a pungent flavour, and a little goes a long way, so you get maximum flavour without removing too much of the plant.

Rosemary likes dry, free-draining conditions, and it will grow in the poorest of soils. So if you have a gap among your paving or by a sunny wall, give it a try. Rosemary can also be propagated easily by taking cuttings (see page 196).

ROSEMARY

THYME

The lovely thing about thyme is that it is a low-growing herb. If allowed to spread, it can creep along the ground creating mounds no higher than about 15cm (6in). There is also a lot of variation to be found in thyme, as it has been bred to have different scents and flavours, as well as flowers and foliage in many colours.

Most, though not all, thyme has variegated foliage. This variegation can be either white or yellow and even sometimes has hints of pink and purple. The flowers are generally mauve or purple, and as such are offset beautifully by the foliage. One of the most beloved varieties of this herb is lemon thyme, which has a delicate citrus tang and rich yellow foliage with bottle-green variegation. This variety is relatively robust looking, yet it still retains a delicate form typical of thymes generally.

As with other Mediterranean herbs, a free-draining, sunny position is best. If you have a tree in a pot, consider growing some thyme at its base – it looks a lot prettier than bare soil, and will cascade a little over the edge of the pot to soften it, while acting as a weed suppressant and conserving moisture for the tree – basically, it acts as a living mulch.

SAGE

Traditional sage (*Salvia officinalis*) grows best in a well drained and sunny position and needs to be cut back in spring, making sure you do not cut back into the old (brown) wood. It can be propagated easily from softwood cuttings and replaced for free when the older plants have become leggy. This is a great grown in pots but make sure that you incorporate enough drainage!

PURPLE SAGE

Sage is a fairly unremarkable-looking plant but there is a plethora of varieties and species that make wonderful ornamentals. The main edible sage that is used as an ornamental alternative is 'Purpurascens', which is exactly like its green cousin only with a beautiful purple foliage, and there are also variegated forms readily available. There are numerous other *Salvia* species that are not edible but have beautiful flowers of varying colours, some of which are extremely intense, so are great to bring in pollinators. Be aware when buying *Salvias* that a lot of them are not hardy so will need replacing every year unless they are brought indoors. You can identify a *Salvia* by its square stems, its alternately opposite foliage and its scent. The flowers themselves are not scented but the foliage nearly always will be.

PARSLEY

This is a great herb, mainly because it is so easy to grow and so versatile. In terms of aesthetics, parsley is nothing special but it is inoffensive and with delicate, toothed leaves it makes a good complementary plant for something more striking.

It grows in partial shade as well as full sun and needs a little more water than most Mediterranean herbs, making it good for temperate climates. It is also a totally herbaceous plant so never gets any woody growth and can be cut back quite hard to then regrow. It will probably need to be replaced annually, though it can sometimes survive a winter but will often look a little worse for wear afterwards.

CORIANDER

Coriander is another truly herbaceous plant that is similar looking to parsley but has an incredibly fresh flavour that lends itself much more to exotic dishes and works fantastically well with lime. The lovely thing about coriander is that you can also use its seeds, which have a much more punchy and spicy flavour.

The main thing you really need to know when growing this herb is that it does not respond well when transplanted, so sow your seeds in shallow drills, at a depth of about 1cm (0.5in), in their final position. That position should be in the sun but if possible should provide a little gentle shade from the midday sun. Once the plants have germinated, thin them out to about 20cm (8in) apart and vigilantly remove any flowers when they form.

FENNEL

Fennel does so much that it just has to feature on my shortlist. Every year it comes back stronger than before and in a single year it can put on up to two metres' growth. It forms tall, sturdy stems topped with delicate umbels of yellow flowers and bright green, feathery foliage. It also comes in a beautiful bronze variety, which isn't quite as vigorous but makes a nice alternative for a smaller space.

Fennel could not be easier to maintain. It grows in most positions but prefers open ground to containers, needs a little sun and should be cut back in autumn. After a

FENNEL

few years in a position that the fennel likes it may become a bit of a monster. You can then give it a 'Chelsea chop', taking off a third of the growth in mid-spring.

OREGANO

This perennial is a great herb. It has hundreds of tiny pink or purple flowers with dark, showy bracts and a headily scented leaf. As a subshrub it will grow back year on year and needs cutting only once, in early spring, when the old flowering stems should be removed. Put it in a sunny, free-draining position and feed with mulch in winter. It will flourish in a container with enough drainage.

MARJORAM

A generous herb that forms a lush shrub, marjoram is a favourite for appearance and taste but mainly for its scent. Marjoram has a similar habit and requires the same kind of care as oregano.

The plant itself is not particularly striking but forms a lush mound with neat leaves that are quite large compared to other culinary herbs and therefore makes a great backdrop against other herbs or plants. Golden marjoram is a particularly nice specimen with a more vibrant, greeny yellow colour than classic marjoram. Do not be fooled by its plain exterior, this is a plant that is well worth growing.

Super
grow

CHAPTER 7
PLANTING & MAINTENANCE

By the time you get to the planting stage, you should have completed all of the hard landscaping. The patio, paths, walls, fences, pond, pergola and any other hard landscape features should be in place, leaving only borders of bare soil (and, perhaps, any plants that the previous occupants left behind that you'd like to keep). By now you'll be itching to plant up your new borders, but don't just yet, as the soil won't be ready. Chances are that it will have been trampled all over during the hard landscape construction and become extremely compacted. There may well be remnants of cement in it that need removing, as well as weeds, large stones, roots and general rubbish. You'll need to dig really well and probably add plenty of organic matter before planting. The soil is the life blood of the garden – if you give it a helping hand and TLC in the early stages it will pay dividends later, making a huge difference to the health of your plants.

JOSEPH BENTLEY

DIG OVER THE SITE

If you've created a new border from scratch, digging through the soil before planting is vital. It allows you to break up hard lumps of earth, dislodge stones and remove weeds, all of which will improve drainage and help plants to put down deep roots, establish themselves and grow strong. Digging also enables you to work the all-important organic matter into the soil (see page 192).

DIGGING TIPS

- It's generally best to use a large garden spade for digging unless you're cultivating heavy clay soil, in which case use a lighter border spade, otherwise the work will be backbreaking. If the soil is in good condition, you may be able to get away with using a garden fork.
- Avoid digging when the soil is wet and heavy, for instance during or after rain, as it can cause the soil to compact and also makes digging much more difficult.
- As you dig, remove any rubble, stones, litter, plant roots and any other bulky undesirables from the soil. The presence of these will at best interrupt the root growth of your plants and at worst cause some toxicity in the soil.
- When breaking up the soil you want to create a 'crumb' texture, which means the clumps of soil are ideally 3–5mm (0.125–0.25in) wide.
- Add plenty of organic matter as you go, unless the soil is waterlogged.

Assess the situation

First things first – avoid doing more than you need to. There is digging and there is double digging, and believe me if you can dodge double digging then you should! Digging to a spade's depth (single digging) should be sufficient on most reasonable soil, but where the soil has never been cultivated, is full of rubble or is poorly drained, double digging may be necessary, as it loosens any compaction and increases fertility and aeration. If you plan to grow vegetables, it is also a good idea to double dig, as it will make the plants grow faster and be more productive.

Start by digging a small hole to investigate the state of your soil after all that trampling. If it's compacted – when the soil sticks together to make a surface impenetrable to a plant's roots – you have some double digging in store. Be aware that your soil may look good on the surface but deeper down it may be compacted. Check beyond a spade blade's depth, and if you hit a solid barrier of compacted soil (known as an 'iron pan') you'll need to double dig.

How to dig

There is a specific method to digging and it pays to do it properly. Single digging is described here. Double digging follows the same method but involves digging the top layer of soil to the depth of two spade blades.

1 Dig a trench to the depth and width of a spade blade. Pile the soil you have removed into a wheelbarrow.

2 Dig a second trench immediately next to the first, breaking the soil into a crumb texture as you do so and adding organic matter. Use this soil/organic matter mixture to fill the first trench.

3 Continue digging in this way all along the bed until you get to the final trench.

4 Fill your final trench with the soil in the wheelbarrow, having mixed in some organic matter first.

5 Go over the whole area and break up clumps with a fork.

Once you've completed the digging you'll need to tread lightly over the soil. The purpose of this is to close up any large pockets of air that may have emerged between the clumps of soil; if the gaps are too large, water won't adhere to the soil. Walk in tiny steps across the entire surface of the border you've just dug. You'll probably find that even after this the surface of the soil will be higher than it was and will stick up above the bed, but don't worry – it will find its level again in time.

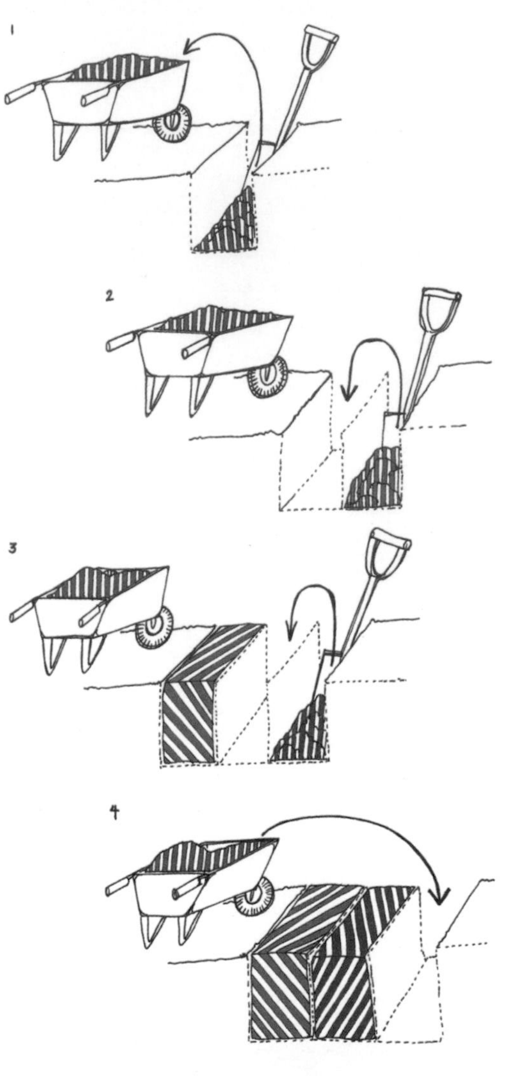

NO DIG METHOD

Some people prefer what is called a 'no dig' policy, which means that you add organic matter to the soil surface and leave the work to nature rather than digging, as worms and other small garden organisms will mix it into the soil over time. This is fine if you've inherited good soil, but if you find that it's compacted or suffering from any of the aforementioned problems, I would certainly recommend a preliminary dig, even if you would prefer to adopt a no dig policy once the border is established.

REMOVING WEEDS

Weeds are the bane of any gardener's life, and when you move into your own place and are undertaking clearance work they become even more of an irritation. There is an old gardeners' saying, 'A year of seeds, seven years of weeds', meaning if you let weeds go to seed for even one season, those seeds will germinate year after year.

There are two kinds of weed – annual and perennial. Annual weeds, such as chickweed or cleavers (goosegrass), will not grow back, so are fairly harmless; you can just bury these as you dig. However, perennial weeds, such as bindweed, ground elder, dandelion and brambles, always need removing. If you dig them in they will proliferate, either by seed or their roots, stems or leaves will spread along the ground, taking up whatever space is available. Some perennial weeds have even been known to grow through concrete and undermine the structure of a house.

Dig out as much of the plant as you possibly can, including the whole root if possible. It really is worth spending time trying to eliminate them before you plant anything. Turn the soil over repeatedly, and remove every bit of weed root or shoot you see. It's a real challenge, and there are bound to be some remaining, but where this is the case try to keep an eye out for the reappearance of any weeds, and pull them out as soon as you see them; over time (and I mean years) this will weaken the plant to a point where it will no longer be able to grow back.

Some gardeners pull out as much as they can of the plant then cover the ground with a weed-suppressing and light-excluding membrane, which weakens the plant as it can no longer photosynthesise. But this won't eliminate the most pernicious of these weeds.

Finally, you can apply a weedkiller to the re-growth in very much the same way you would apply it to a lawn, but do this with caution. For starters, the weed has to be just the right size when the chemical is applied: if the plant is too large, the weedkiller won't work; if it's too small, the weed can often recover. Usually, it's recommended that the plant is around a few inches tall and has a few sets of leaves. It's also important to follow the instructions on the bottle and apply it in the right conditions – it mustn't be too hot, cold, rainy or windy. These conditions will cause the chemicals to evaporate, not work effectively, get washed off or get blown onto other plants that you may want to keep. It's best to spray in the morning, in spring or summer, on a calm day. Always be considerate to wildlife when using such products as some contain toxins that are damaging to animals, and combine it with digging out the weeds. Do not expect a weedkiller to do the whole job for you.

There's no getting rid of weeds without a bit of hard work, but that is one of the reasons I enjoy gardening. The hard work is really rewarding, and you'll achieve a lot more after an hour's digging than you think – especially if you have someone on hand to make regular cups of tea!

ADDING SOIL IMPROVERS

The ideal garden soil is fertile and free-draining but water-retentive. Unfortunately, not all of us are blessed with this. Your garden may have a very chalky or heavy clay soil (see page 18), and/or it may have been badly neglected by the previous owners. You'll improve the texture of your soil to some extent by just digging and/or forking over the soil. However, to make substantial improvements to soil texture, moisture retention, drainage or fertility, soil improvers are a must.

Organic matter

When I was studying for my horticulture degree, there was a joke among the soil scientists that any problem can be solved by the addition of organic matter – and in most cases this is true. Nearly all soils are improved by adding this magic ingredient. Organic matter comes in various forms – well-rotted farm manure, garden compost, leaf mould, spent mushroom compost, and so on. It's best to avoid peat, as it is not considered environmentally friendly.

The benefits of organic matter are numerous: it helps dry soils to hold on to moisture and chalky, sandy or silty soils to retain nutrients, and aerates heavy clay or compacted soils. It also encourages worms, which are invaluable in the garden.

The only time you don't want to use organic matter is when the soil is waterlogged, as it can encourage a build-up of methane and other toxic substances. If you have a peaty soil that is often waterlogged (and a clue that indicates you have that problem is a sulphurous smell coming from the soil) then adding organic matter to it will not do any good. Far better would be to incorporate some kind of drainage system and sand or gravel to help prevent the water from sitting for long periods in the soil.

Other soil improvers

If you have a heavy clay or waterlogged soil, to improve drainage dig coarse horticultural sand, gravel or grit into the soil every now and again, particularly during the winter months.

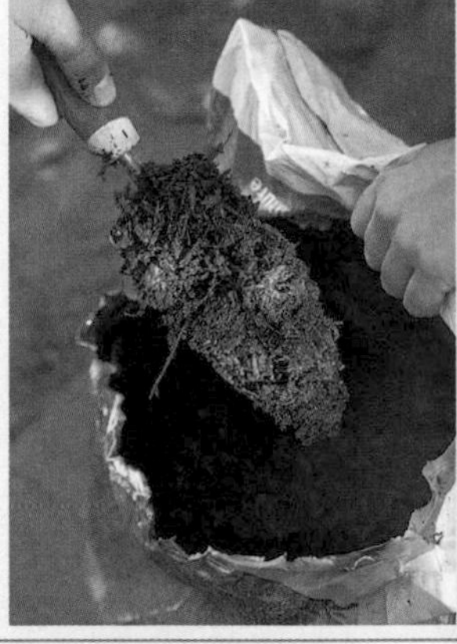

Although I try to avoid chemicals, I find if a soil is low in nutrients it helps to feed it with a chemical fertiliser. When adding nutrients, think about what plant you want to grow and the nutrients it needs. The main nutrients are: nitrogen (N) for shoot and leaf growth; phosphorus (P) for root growth; and potassium (K) for fruit and flowers. The packet containing the fertiliser should state the N:P:K ratio in the product, so you can decide which one is right for your particular plant's needs.

GREEN MANURES

If you have a heavy clay soil or a waterlogged soil, you may find that manure makes it too heavy or even more waterlogged. Instead, try growing a green manure for a season and then digging that into the soil. You can buy seed packets of green manure including mustard, clover, peas or beans. All legumes are nitrogen fixing, which means that they make the nitrogen in the soil available to plants and also add more nitrogen. I would really recommend this as a good method of fertiliser, particularly as most of these plants are great for encouraging wildlife.

ALTERING THE SOIL PH

While you can slightly alter the pH of your soil, for instance by adding lime to make a soil less acidic, it is not recommended. No solution is permanent, and if you're continually adding lime to the soil, for example, it becomes a delicate balancing act and also becomes quite expensive. Remember, there is no point in labouring needlessly trying to make plants grow in a position where they're unhappy. You can mollycoddle them into mild contentment sometimes, but really a plant will only flourish where it's happiest. For plants that cope with highly acidic or alkaline sites, see pages 20–21.

PLANTING BASICS

When you plant there are a few key things that make the job quicker, easier, and more effective. Of course planting is simple but with a little know-how you can do it like a professional and make your garden instantly stunning and ensure that you grow happy, healthy plants.

1. First things first, plants need to have moist roots before they go in the ground. It is a good idea to soak them before planting, and if planting a tree, soak it for at least an hour.

2. The next thing is to make the soil as easily accessible for the plants as you can. If you have improved your soil then this should be done already, but for extra success, always dig the ground before planting and make sure the hole you make is nice and generous (at least a third wider than the existing root ball).

Before you remove any soil from the hole, give it a good dig so that all the soil you do dig out has a fine tilth and can be easily swept back in without running the risk of any big clods breaking stems. Never bury a plant deeper than it was buried in the pot. Plants have a preferred depth and planting them too deep can rot the stems. It is particularly important to remember this with trees as, unlike other perennials, they cannot quickly change their habits to accommodate any uncomfortable planting positions.

3. Before the plant goes in the ground make sure that it is free of weeds and pests and that any dead or diseased parts are removed. You might want to think about adding mycorrhizal spores to the roots as this promotes healthy root growth in the soil. Otherwise mixing in a little feed to the surrounding soil can help.

4. If the roots are too tightly bound in the pot, then break them up or tease them out to release them so that they can explore through the soil and find nutrients and water. Otherwise they are what is called 'pot bound' and end up circling round and round, strangling themselves, never getting the nutrients they need and never managing to anchor themselves in the ground effectively.

5. When you have put the plant in the ground and filled up the hole with soil, firm the earth with either your heel or your hands. After that, rough over the soil with your fingertips to level it. This will give a professional and neat finish.

FINALLY...

Water the plant in well so that the water soaks all the way to the bottom of the roots and further. The last thing you want to do is only water the surface because that encourages roots to grow up to the surface rather than exploring down into the soil.

You may want to stake a newly planted tree to ensure it stays in its position. Face the stake into the prevailing wind and hammer it in at an angle of about 45 degrees. Never fix a stake to a tree higher than a third of the way up its stem as the movement of the crown will encourage the trunk to thicken and the tree to become stronger.

Keep new plants moist during their first few weeks and once they have established, reduce watering to encourage them to survive on their own.

When planting anything, always check how big it will eventually grow and plant with enough space between plants to allow them to grow to their full size without encroaching on the other plants around them.

MAKING CUTTINGS

The main thing to remember with cuttings is that the plant you end up with will be a clone of the plant that you cut it from. You can prune it to be a different shape but its genes will be the same. So keep that in mind and only choose parts of the plant that show it at its best.

1. Remove a growing tip from the plant by cutting it off just above a node – this where the leaves join the main stem. Always look for healthy, typical, non-flowering stems whenever possible. Cut the removed piece of foliage just below the leaf joint above. There is concentrated plant hormone at a node with the potential to become roots as the cutting develops.

2. Remove all the lower foliage either by pinching it off or using clean secateurs. This reduces water loss and makes for more successful cuttings.

3. Pinch out the growing tip. This is not always necessary but usually this promotes a more bushy habit rather than a long, leggy plant.

4. Prepare a pot with seed and cutting compost and make a hole in the compost with either your finger or a dibber. You can put more than one cutting in a pot if you are pushed for space but they will need separating once they put on root growth.

5. Place the cutting in the hole and firm it in. Then give it a good soak, preferably by placing it in a tray of water. In some instances you may find that cuttings strike more successfully if you use something called hormone rooting powder. This is more effective on woody cuttings but can be helpful on softwood cuttings as a fungicide. You may find that you have more successful cuttings by placing them right up against the side of the pot – this makes the cutting warmer, but can make the root growth lopsided. Try both ways if you have never done it before.

PLANTING SEEDS

The bigger the seed, the deeper it should be planted. So for really tiny seeds, just sprinkling them on the surface of the soil is fine. There are a few key rules to successful seed sowing: use seed and cutting compost; remember that seeds need to be kept moist and always keep them warm. Sometimes you can germinate them in a plastic bag or even a propagator and then remove them once the leaves start to show. Pot seedlings on once their true leaves start to show. Finally, don't just throw them outside once they are big enough. The shock of the cold could actually finish them off. Gradually acclimatise them to the outside temperatures.

BASIC PLANT CARE

Watering

When plants are in containers they will need regular watering, sometimes once a day in the high season. Plants in the borders, though, should only need watering when it is exceptionally dry. If you have chosen plants that will tolerate their environment, they should be well suited to the amount of water they get. If you water them too much after they have become established, they will become dependent and when something like a hosepipe ban or dry spell occurs, you find they all turn up their toes at the drop of a hat. By not watering them you encourage the roots to find water deep in the soil and reduce their dependence on regular watering. Also water soil directly and avoid watering the foliage.

Feeding

Again, you should keep your feeding regime to a minimum, not least because it will become an incredibly expensive business. As with the watering, containers will require regular feeding to keep them at their best. The most hungry (and indeed thirsty) plants are fruits and vegetables – the quality of crops that have been deprived of water and nutrients will be poor. But other than that you should only have to feed a couple of times a year with manure or comfrey tea and the application of chemical fertilisers on your ornamentals should be unnecessary. The best thing you can do is improve your soil in the winter with a good dose of manure or compost and then give a rejuvenating scattering of organic fertiliser on the beds in the spring or early summer.

Deadheading

Not all plants will repeat flower and many produce beautiful seed heads. For such species deadheading is unnecessary. For the rest, however, deadheading throughout the summer months will keep your plants producing flowers, sometimes right up until the first frosts. Do not simply cut the flower off but take the cut right down to the next set of buds or leaves. That way you are not left with ugly spikes sticking up all over the place.

With annuals, it is worth leaving some flowers on towards the end of the season so that you can collect some of the seed for next year's displays. Using seed like this will save you a lot of money. You may find that the plants are more varied than the hybrids you buy (especially with vegetables) but that can add to their charm. If you are relying on a crop for food then it is sometimes best to repurchase the seed each year and in such cases you will want to deadhead right through to the autumn because in cases like these deadheading is better known as harvesting (removing the seeds before they fully mature)!

Cutting back

Perennials will need cutting back once a year. Most of them will need to be cut back in the autumn or winter but some (the ones that flower in the spring or the winter) will need to be cut back once they have finished flowering and started to die off.

Generally cut back to, or just above, the crown. If in doubt leave a few inches of stem on the plant. For tender perennials, leave a little extra on to offer some protection against frost. Alternatively, cut them back when the frost risk has dissipated.

Division

Division is usually done in the autumn, with a few exceptions. The exact method will vary depending on the species. Some produce runners that are like miniature, separate plants that can be pulled off easily and potted up while others will form dense roots that can only be divided with a spade and some considerable force. Other root systems can be prized apart and others will be done with two forks pushed into the roots and then pulled apart. The basic idea is that when plants become big, they can start to produce fewer flowers, so if you break them up and then replant them, you reinvigorate the growth while simultaneously multiplying your collection and filling your garden.

Winter protection

Winter protection will vary according to species. Some will need none and can be exposed to all the elements, while others will need extensive constructions built around them in order to guarantee successful overwintering. With most perennials, the best thing to do is to cover them with a mulch. A mulch is a layer of something that keeps water from evaporating, suppresses weeds and can eventually feed the ground beneath it. It also keeps the temperature up so that the plants are offered protection from frost. The downside is that mulch also offers protection for insects so pests can overwinter successfully too. In wet winters a mulch can also cause some drought-tolerant plants to rot. Apply a mulch if a plant is a little tender but do not apply to all plants indiscriminately. To protect really tender plants, bring them inside if they are in containers, or put them into a greenhouse. Otherwise you will need to keep the frost off with a physical barrier. Straw is traditionally used for this and wool is very good too; because it does not get as wet it causes less rotting. Horticultural fleece is designed just for this purpose. It can be wrapped around tender plants or pinned on the soil above the crowns to keep the frost off.

Pests and diseases

Every plant has different pests and diseases that will affect it. For prized specimens, learn the pests and diseases that affect them and keep a close look out for them. For more general control, keep your plants healthy to reduce the risk of an attack having any devastating effects. It also helps to try to maintain a healthy balance of all kinds of wildlife so that no one species gets too dominant in the food chain and pests and diseases are killed off by each other.

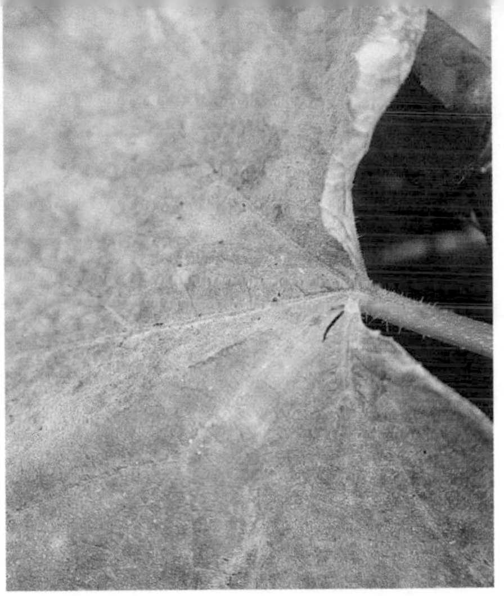

Always keep an eye out for anything that looks unhealthy, investigate it and remove and incinerate any affected material. In the event of a bad infestation or infection you may want to turn to chemical solutions. You should research these according to the species, disease or pest. Remember that moist and warm conditions are the most likely to promote diseases, both bacterial and fungal. A good pruning regime will make a world of difference to plant health.

Basic pruning

Look out for any damaged, dead, infected or infested stems, branches and leaves and remove them as soon as you can. Remove any branches or stems that cross, or rub on each other cause wounds that can become a weak point open for infection.

Always cut just above a node (leaf joint) otherwise the stem above the cut will die back, opening up the plant to infection. Always make diagonal cuts that slope away from the leaf joint. This way water slides off the cut and does not have a chance to rot the plant.

Try to promote an open habit with your pruning. Think of the ideal shape as a martini glass rather than a brandy one. You want the branches and stems to grow away from one another so that the air can move easily through the centre of the plant and keep things fresh.

EARLY SPRING

As the days get longer and brighter, and the weather warms up a little, you'll begin to see small changes in the garden. This is a magical time of year, full of the promise of the season ahead. Snowdrops and daffodils begin to poke their heads through the soil and produce their cheery little flowers, and yellows, blues and fresh green dominate the garden scene. Temperatures can still be on the nippy side, and frosts are by no means a thing of the past, so make sure you provide frost protection for vulnerable plants, including seedlings. This is the start of the new gardening year and therefore a busy time for the gardener.

FLOWERS

● Sow summer-flowering hardy annuals. ● Lift and divide overgrown clumps of summer-flowering perennials. ● Cut back winter growth of perennials in areas prone to a late, hard frost. ● Deadhead daffodils as the flowers fade but leave the foliage. ● Divide snowdrops straight after flowering. ● Sow seed of half-hardy annuals and tender perennials under glass. ● Plant out hardy perennials after hardening them off. ● Take the first softwood cuttings from perennials and shrubs.

TREES AND SHRUBS

● Trim evergreens if required. ● Plant evergreen hedges. ● Plant container-grown deciduous trees and shrubs. ● Move evergreen shrubs. ● Finish planting bare-root trees and shrubs. ● Layer evergreen shrubs and herbaceous perennials. ● Prune back forsythias and flowering quince (*Chaenomeles*) once it has finished flowering. ● Give lavender its very last prune before the flowers start to show.

CLIMBERS

● Tie in stems that may have been blown around in winter winds. ● Prune climbers that flower on the current season's growth. ● Prune clematis group 3 (*Herbaceous Clematis*).

VEGETABLES, FRUIT AND HERBS

● Sow globe artichokes, Brussels sprouts and herbs. Sow annuals such as leeks, cabbages, lettuce, early peas, early potatoes, rhubarb and radishes. ● Harvest baby carrots, chard and rocket. ● Finish digging and feeding vegetable beds. ● Give support to fruit trees where required. ● Spray apples and pears to prevent scab. ● Add a little manure around the base of fruit trees if required.

LAWNS

● Sow seed in lawns if conditions aren't too cold or too dry. ● Repair any patches now that might not have taken in autumn. ● Neaten lawn edges. ● Prepare ground for a new lawn. ● Do first mow of the year if the weather is mild. ● Rake grass and mow once for a grass or wildflower meadow. Do not mow again until the end of summer.

PATIOS, CONTAINERS & HARD LANDSCAPE FEATURES

● Repair any frost damage that might have occurred during the winter – for example, concrete might have blown or timber split. ● Clean and prepare surfaces for use throughout the summer to prevent them from becoming too slippery. ● Plant out any spring bedding, bringing it in if frost is forecast.

PONDS AND OTHER WATER FEATURES

● Put the pump back in the pond and remove any pond heaters you may have put in over winter. ● Remove any leaves that have fallen in the pond or remove netting.

PEST, DISEASE AND WEED PATROL

● Search for greenfly and if visible spray with either a pesticide or washing-up liquid. ● Keep a watchful eye and remove any pests as and when they are seen on your vegetables. ● Hoe weed seedlings from the ground as they start to emerge.

MID-SPRING TO EARLY SUMMER

By now the growing season is in full swing. The frosts have all but gone and the garden landscape is ever changing. Bulbs are king at this time of year. We still see many blues and yellows, but you'll begin to see more purples and pinks – alliums, camassias, tulips and cherry blossom, which really steal the show during the spring, as well as roses, which take up the mantle and flower from late spring right through summer. It's all about the flowers at this time of year, but in terms of maintenance it's one of the quietest times, so sit back and enjoy your outdoor space. There's no harvesting, no clearing, no desperately trying to keep everything under control. Apart from a little clipping and neatening, you really can let the garden take care of itself.

FLOWERS ● Cut a third of the growth off any late-flowering perennials such as asters, sedums, anthemis, solidago, heleniums and phlox. ● Plant out non-hardy plants, such as begonias, pelargoniums, lobelia, cannas and dahlias, once the risk of frost has passed. ● Plant out tender summer bulbs. ● Deadhead spring bulbs as they go over. ● Start staking any flowers on long, potentially floppy stems, before they grow too strongly. ● Remove any spent foliage from bulbs and remove seed heads, so the plants can conserve their energy for next year.

TREES AND SHRUBS ● Prune *Aucuba japonica* and *Berberis*. ● Cut off any frost-damaged stems and branches ● Plant container-grown trees and shrubs. ● Water newly planted trees in dry weather .● Clip box hedges.

CLIMBERS ● Tie in unruly shoots as required.

VEGETABLES, FRUIT AND HERBS ● Plant out marigolds and nasturtiums as companion plants to vegetables and fruit. ● Thin out seedlings of parsnips, beetroot, carrots and leeks where necessary. ● Harvest first radishes and lettuce and continue harvesting. ● Earth up potatoes. ● In later spring sow: maincrop peas, beans, beet and parsnips, maincrop potatoes, carrots, spinach, kale and seakale. ● Regularly water and feed all vegetable and fruit plants and remove weeds using a hoe. ● Sow winter vegetables for the coming autumn, including runner beans, broccoli, winter and Savoy cabbage, kale and marrows. ● Hand-pollinate any fruit blossoms with a paintbrush to ensure successful pollination.

LAWNS ● Weed the lawn. ● Mow regularly. ● Lay turf. Make sure newly laid turf is kept moist. ● Fertilise the lawn sporadically using your preferred method.

PATIOS, CONTAINERS & HARD LANDSCAPE FEATURES ● Spring clean the shed. ● Regularly feed and water containers. ● Feed bulbs in containers once the flowers have finished but the foliage is still there. This makes them stronger for next year. ● Change container displays once early spring bulbs have gone over.

PONDS AND OTHER WATER FEATURES ● Divide crowded or overgrown aquatic plants. ● Introduce new plants and reintroduce any that were removed over winter.

PEST, DISEASE AND WEED PATROL ● Net around fruit trees to protect the blossoms and the fruits from being eaten by birds. ● Watch for beetles, blackfly and caterpillars, and spray against aphids. ● Check regularly for root pests like wireworm and vine weevil.

MIDSUMMER

After your relaxing spring, this is when the hard work really starts, and it doesn't stop until the winter as far as the plants are concerned. The frost risk should now be over, so those plants that have been nurtured through winter and spring should be outside. The flowers will be in full bloom and you'll find that you can start harvesting some produce now, too.

FLOWERS

● Hoe and weed regularly. ● Continue staking plants. ● Deadhead flowers regularly so they will repeat flower, except where the plants produce seed heads that are attractive or useful for wildlife. ● Plant autumn-flowering bulbs. ● Plant out any unplanted bedding. ● Take softwood or semi ripe cuttings from perennials, place them in a protected area and keep well watered. ● Start collecting seed heads for next year's sowing. ● Think about which flowering shrubs might need a prune.

TREES AND SHRUBS

● Clip yew hedges. ● Give wisteria its first prune (see page 143). ● Prune early spring-flowering shrubs. ● Take semi-ripe cuttings. ● Pot on any softwood cuttings. ● Trim conifer hedges.

CLIMBERS

● Harvest passionflower fruits.

VEGETABLES, FRUIT AND HERBS

● Regularly feed and water vegetables, particularly cucumbers. ● Keep an eye open for tomato problems. ● Stop your climbing beans by pinching out the tops if they start to get too high. ● Harvest kale, cabbage, peas and beans, tomatoes, spinach, peppers, broccoli and cauliflower. Continue harvesting lettuce, rocket and chard. ● Apply grease bands to the trunks of grapevines, *Euonymus*, *Rhododendron* and *Liquidambar* and keep doing so throughout the autumn to stop wingless female pests laying eggs in the tree's branches. ● Sow spring cabbage, turnips (for roots at the beginning of this season and for tops a month or so later), red cabbage and cauliflowers. ● Start ripening your onions: bend over the tops once most have collapsed on their own and lost colour. Leave the onions in for a further 10 days–2 weeks then pull them out of the ground on a sunny day. Leave them in the sun for a day or two and then bring them in (preferably not during or straight after rain as this will make them go soft more quickly). ● Harvest raspberries, cherries, some plums, beans, peas, tomatoes and many more. ● Earth up celery and leeks.

LAWNS

● Mow a spring-flowering wildflower meadow to prevent tough grasses from becoming too overbearing to the delicate spring flowers. ● For a 'bowling-green-style' lawn, continue to mow regularly. In very dry conditions, you may need to water too though, try to keep this to an absolute minimum. ● Remove any lawn weeds before they have a chance to set seed.

PATIOS, CONTAINERS & HARD LANDSCAPE FEATURES

● Keep containers well watered. ● If you have a greenhouse, provide a form of shading to prevent plants scorching in the sun and drying out. Add shutters or blinds, or use greenhouse shading paint, which can be applied using a brush or sprayer. ● In really hot weather, move plants away from a south-facing wall or to a shadier spot so that they don't scorch.

PONDS AND OTHER WATER FEATURES

● Top up ponds in hot weather. ● Plant new aquatics. ● Remove blanket weed and algae.

PEST, DISEASE AND WEED PATROL

● Watch out for silver leaf on fruit. ● Keep an eye open for mildew on ornamentals and vegetables. Prevent it occurring by watering in the morning and making sure the plants do not get too damp, being especially careful to avoid watering the foliage (see page 198). ● Look for leatherjackets in the lawn – largish brown grubs, which cause yellow patches in the grass. To treat, water the grass then cover it with thick polythene. Gather up the grubs as they come to the surface.

LATE SUMMER

The flowers that come to the fore at the end of summer can be bigger, brighter and bolder than earlier flowers and can really give the garden a new lease of life. However, they do take quite a bit of maintenance. If you don't have hours to spend tending to your borders, you might find that the garden starts to look a little bit tired at this point. If that happens, don't let it get you down – remember, flowers are not a prerequisite in the garden, and letting things go to seed is good for wildlife. Just make sure you harvest regularly and tie back plants where needed to give a tidier effect – stakes and string work wonders, and tying back takes only a few minutes.

FLOWERS

● Staking is crucial now. The increased wind levels mean that if you don't stake, you'll find more and more plants blowing over and the garden will look messy. ● Collect seeds for sowing next year or scatter them around the borders. ● Consider stopping deadheading. Frosted seed heads look stunning and provide winter sustenance for birds. ● Start lifting and potting any half-hardy and tender plants. ● Cut back any perennials that have died back. ● Take cuttings from pelargoniums (non-flowering stems). ● Buy your bulbs for next season. Plant them if you like but this can wait until the autumn, provided they are kept in a cool, dry place.

TREES AND SHRUBS

● Trees and shrubs mostly take care of themselves at this time of year. Watch out for heavily laden branches falling in those early late-summer winds. ● Neaten any messy growth on hedges.

CLIMBERS

● Immediately after flowering, prune all climbers that flower on the previous year's growth. ● Prune rambling roses. ● Prune honeysuckle with lots of dead wood in it once it has finished flowering.

VEGETABLES, FRUIT AND HERBS

● Harvest, harvest, harvest. Apart from a few specific, winter vegetables, now is the time when you will find your kitchen garden at its most prolific. Dig it all up and eat it. (Apart from legumes, which should be pulled out and the nitrogen-fixing root nodules left in the ground for the winter.) ● Store surplus fruit and vegetables. ● Plan next year's crops and rotation. ● Cut down asparagus and lift tubers to dry store. ● Harvest the majority of plum varieties and prune plum trees. ● Sow winter lettuce and spinach.

LAWNS

● Start mowing a summer-flowering wildflower meadow. Wait for all your summer flowers to finish and set seed, then start mowing until autumn. ● Keep regularly feeding and mowing the lawn. ● Seed lawn and repair any patches with seed and compost. Protect from the birds! ● Start removing worm casts from the lawn and beware of mowing in excessive dew.

PATIOS, CONTAINERS & HARD LANDSCAPE FEATURES

● Bring in tender plants and start planning autumn and winter pot displays. ● Clean down patios and decked areas, especially if they are under sycamore or lime trees as they will be very sticky.

PONDS AND OTHER WATER FEATURES

● Thin oxygenators and floating plants. ● Deadhead flowers to stop seeding.

PEST, DISEASE AND WEED PATROL

● Remove any foliage that has been affected by disease in the summer, such as mildew or black spot on roses. As with any diseased material, avoid putting the leaves on the compost. The best thing to do is incinerate them. ● Keep removing aphids, slugs, snails, grubs and mites wherever you see them. The more you get now, the fewer will overwinter in the garden and attack next year. ● Cover any remaining fruits with heavy-duty netting to keep birds at bay.

AUTUMN

There are few flowers around so leaving seed heads and late flowers is really important for the insects and birds still flying around. As the season goes on the chance of frost is more likely so you may need to start bringing in plants or protecting them on cold nights. You also need to think about cutting back the season's growth, feeding the ground and tidying up. Plan for next year by planting your bulbs and start sowing seeds for next year's vegetables and flowers.

FLOWERS ● Lift and pot up tender perennials from the borders, including begonias, pelargoniums, cannas, lobelia, gladioli and dahlias. ● Plant bulbs that will flower the following spring, including tulips, daffodils, grape hyacinths (*Muscari*), scillas, hyacinths (*Hyacinthus*), bluebells (*Hyacinthoides*), alliums, camassias and glory of the snow (*Chionodoxa*). Snowdrops (*Galanthus*) need to be purchased 'in the green', as a potful of growing plants still in leaf, rather than as dry bulbs. ● Plan and make your borders for the following year and start buying seeds of annuals and perennials. Sow them according to the instructions; most can be sown in autumn.

TREES AND SHRUBS ● Protect plants from frost if required. ● Cut back perennials that have gone over. ● Divide perennials. ● Deadhead any flowers that are still going but start leaving seeds and hips on those that are coming to an end, either for decoration during the winter months or to feed wildlife. ● If it's frosty or unseasonably cold, leave some of the season's material on the plant and leave cutting back until spring, to protect the crown of the plant. ● Towards the end of autumn, root-prune trees and shrubs that have got too big. ● Layer deciduous plants. ● Mulch borders with organic matter. ● Collect leaves from beneath trees where they have been shed and either put on the compost or create a humus-rich leaf mould. ● Prune *Abelia, Hydrangea, Cotinus* and *Laburnum*. ● Sow acers, box (*Buxus*), junipers (*Juniperus*), lavender (*Lavandula*), rosemary (*Rosmarinus*), viburnums and hollies (*Ilex*). ● Prune lavender (*Lavandula*), being careful not to cut into old wood.

CLIMBERS ● Plant out vines and other bare-rooted climbers. ● Tie in and train long, unruly shoots.

VEGETABLES, FRUIT AND HERBS ● Plant bare-rooted fruit trees. ● Propagate all currants. ● Prune black cherry, fig, raspberry and peach. ● Remove foliage from strawberry plants to allow next year's buds to form. ● Add manure to currants and other fruiting shrubs. ● Apply wood ash to the base of fruiting trees and shrubs to promote a high yield the following season. ● Harvest and preserve the last of the fruit.

LAWNS ● After the last mow of the year, scarify, aerate and top-dress the lawn (see page 73). ● Regularly remove fallen leaves and worm casts from the surface. (These are both really good to put into compost, or you could make leaf mould with the leaves.) ● Repair any bare patches with grass seed on top of a dressing of lawn sand and compost. ● Top-dress the lawn with lawn sand (see page 73).

PATIOS, CONTAINERS & HARD LANDSCAPE FEATURES ● Treat timber with preservative to give it protection for the coming winter. ● Remove dead plants from containers and replace compost. Plant any spring bulbs for the next season in containers. Tulip bulbs will need to be replaced every three or so years. ● Start planning any hard landscape construction or re-levelling to be completed during the coming winter.

PONDS AND OTHER WATER FEATURES ● Remove decomposing material to stop build-up of nitrates. ● Trim back oxygenators. ● Remove any tender plants to overwinter under cover. ● Remove and clean pumps, filters and fountains.

PEST, DISEASE AND WEED PATROL ● Clean stakes and tools. ● Pick up leaves that may be harbouring larvae and grubs, as well as eggs, so that there is less chance of those pests coming back the following spring.

WINTER

As temperatures plummet, plants will now be fully dormant and even the earliest and toughest of species won't brave sticking their heads above the soil until the first signs of spring. This means there isn't a lot to do in terms of plant maintenance. However, winter is the best time to undertake hard landscaping projects – the clear ground will give you a really good sense of your space, making the design process easier, and you're less likely to trample on and damage plants. The great thing about winter is it can be a period of relaxation or great productivity.

FLOWERS ● Protect tender and half-hardy plants. ● Sow and plant: alstromerias, begonias, pinks (*Dianthus*), anemones, snapdragons (*Antirrhinum*), asters, cosmos, dahlias, fuchsias, lobelia, scabious (*Scabiosa*) and salvias. Protect under glass if necessary. ● Remove any seed heads that are looking scruffy and expose winter-flowering plants like hellebores and snowdrops (*Galanthus*) to the light by removing bits of the foliage or messy leaves of surrounding plants. ● Take root cuttings of perennials such as comfrey. ● Plant snowdrops while they have leaves. You may also want to divide them. ● In cold areas, leave last year's plant material on for longer to protect the crowns.

TREES AND SHRUBS ● Plant bare-root trees and shrubs. ● Root-prune trees and shrubs. ● Take hardwood cuttings from woody shrubs and trees. Protect under glass. ● Remove any dead material, rotten branches and crossing branches and generally tidy any trees and shrubs that have become overgrown. ● Protect non-hardy species from frost.

CLIMBERS ● Remove any dead material and tie in stems that are getting unruly. ● Check ties, hooks, wires and other supports holding your climbers to the wall or fence. Replace these if they are beginning to fall apart. ● Give wisteria its second prune (see page 143). ● Prune climbing roses and feed with a healthy spade-full of manure around the base. ● Plant bare-root climbing and rambler roses.

VEGETABLES, FRUIT AND HERBS ● Prepare seedbeds. ● Prune fruit trees and shrubs, including gooseberries, currants, apples, pears and cherries. Prune grapevines in the depth of the cold season. ● Feed soil with manure, compost or green manure, and dig in if required. ● Sow onions, parsnips and shallots straight into the soil and cauliflower and beans under glass. ● Protect apple, cherry, plum, pear and berry blossom buds from frost by draping with horticultural fleece. ● Do a pest and disease check on fruit trees when foliage has fallen. Remove any cankers and other disease damage. Spray pesticide if necessary.

LAWNS ● Rake and remove thatch build-up and fallen leaves. ● Neaten edges.

PATIOS, CONTAINERS & HARD LANDSCAPE FEATURES ● Wash any hard landscape features regularly to avoid build-up of moss and algae. ● Construct any big projects while plants are dormant. ● If required, wrap containers in bubble wrap to stop the roots from freezing. ● Make sure your containers do not become waterlogged through the winter – especially if they contain bulbs. If necessary keep them under shelter and do not over water them. ● Take indoors any tender perennials in containers.

PONDS AND OTHER WATER FEATURES ● Install a pond heater or float a ball on the water to prevent the pond from freezing over.

PEST, DISEASE AND WEED PATROL ● Check under flowerpots and in all nooks and crannies for slugs and snails to avoid infestation the following year. ● Remove any leaves, plant material and even soil around plants that were infected in the growing season and incinerate them. ● Clean and sterilise all garden tools.

INDEX

M

N

O

P

R

S

T

U

V

W

Y

ACKNOWLEDGEMENTS

So many people have been so helpful to me during the creation of this, my first book. Firstly I must thank Vicky, my editor, for all her help, and everyone at Kyle Books for giving me the opportunity to do something I never thought I would be capable of. I have loved it, so thank you all so much. Also to Clare, who took the beautiful photographs and Helen, for her wonderful design.

There is one person who I must thank immensely for his support and help with this project and throughout my entire career: Steve Edney, head gardener at The Salutation Gardens – my friend and former tutor. I'm surprised how often your advice still pops into my head and it turns out you were always right!

Thank you Alan Titchmarsh for your support and advice, not just with the book but in everything. It means the world to me.

David Dodd and all at The Outdoor Room (http://www.theoutdoorroom.co.uk/) in West Sussex were also immensely helpful during this project and have become great friends over the last three years. I would also like to thank James Billinghurst at Littlescapes in Bristol (http://www.littlescapes.co.uk/) who worked incredibly hard to help me and whose efforts were invaluable. I could not have made this book without you so thank you. Also a big thank you to Amanda Patton (http://www.amandapatton.co.uk/). You were incredibly helpful and I enjoyed our conversations, not to mention your beautiful garden. Another person who was incredibly helpful during this process was Rosemary Coldstream (http://rosemarycoldstream.com/). Our day in St Albans was great and we could have done it all in just your garden! Also Lesley Hegarty (http://www.hegartywebberpartnership.com/) and Bob Latham (http://www.lathamdesign.co.uk/), Fiona Leaming, Carol Barrows, Richard Hardwick, Lindsay Driscoll, Gemma Murray, Pat and John Lee, Tim Richmond, Amanda Charlton, Richard Merelie, Alan Elm and Grenville Johnson for all of your help when we were in Bristol. The gardens were fantastic.

Thank you also to everybody at Spungold TV for the opportunity you have given me, but especially Matt Young who was so helpful with the book. And thank you to all those in Deal who helped me to get a bit of my childhood home into my book: Linda Worrell, Janet and Jack Turnball, and Georgina, Carrie and Zack Callister (though you don't know it!). Thank you all so much.

Without the support of one person this book would never have been written. So thank you Steve Briers. I owe you one.

I would like to thank my family: Mum, Dad, Bid, Charlie and little Bilfred. You've all been so wonderful throughout everything. I cannot put into words the gratitude I have and the luck I feel that I have you in my life.

Also to all at The Botanics: Phil Lusby, Greg Kenicer and Leigh Morris, who all bent over backwards to accommodate me during the first two years of Love Your Garden and all my fellow students, especially Nick, Cornelia, Fiona, Duncan and Chris. You have been more than supportive and I thank you for everything. The same thanks go to everyone at SRUC. Also Charlie and Neville, style gurus and like family, thank you. I would also like to thank all my friends back in Sandwich (and now spread all over the place) for all of your support over the years. To all these people and many more, a big thank you.